Never Give In

THE EXTRAORDINARY CHARACTER OF WINSTON CHURCHILL

STEPHEN MANSFIELD

GENERAL EDITOR, GEORGE GRANT

LEADERS IN ACTION SERIES

CUMBERLAND HOUSE

PUBLISHING INC.

NEVER GIVE IN
PUBLISHED BY CUMBERLAND HOUSE PUBLISHING, INC.
431 Harding Industrial Drive
Nashville, Tennessee 37211

All Scripture quotations are taken from the *King James Version.*

Library of Congress Cataloging-in-Publication Data
Mansfield, Stephen
    Never give in : the extraordinary character of Winston Churchill / Stephen Mansfield.
        p. cm. — (Leaders in action)
    ISBN 13: 978-1-888952-19-3
    ISBN 1-888952-19-9 (hb alk. paper)
    ISBN 1-58182-322-3 (pb alk. paper)
    1. Churchill, Winston, Sir, 1874–1965. 2. Great Britain—Politics and government—20th century. 3. Prime ministers—Great Britain—Biography. 4. Political leadership. I. Title. II. Series.
DA566.9.C5M273 1995b
941.084'092—dc20   96-27189

Printed in the United States of America

    7 8 9 10—08 07

to my father
for my son

Table of Contents

FOREWORD

By George Grant

The great Scottish author and statesman John Buchan once wrote, "History is neither science nor philosophy, though it enlists both in its service; but it is indisputably an art." Indeed, as a reconstruction of the past, history demands precisely the qualities that we look for in a good novel.

History is, after all, primarily a story. Thus, it ought to have the swiftness and cohesion of a page-turning narrative. It ought to have drama, so that the sequence of events may be shown to issue in some great moment. At the same time, it ought not be encumbered with melodrama. The great moment must not appear as an isolated and fantastic crisis, but rather linked to a long chain of causes inspired by certain protagonists and antagonists. And of course, those protagonists and antagonists ought to be somehow made to live again with something of their original vigor so as to make them recognizable to us as fellow human beings.

Particularly when history is viewed through the focused lens of biography, the past ought not be a mere sketch in pen and ink, after the fashion of our minor modern moralists. Instead, it ought to be a snapshot, with all the shades and halftones of our common life in this poor fallen world. It ought to thus capture for us a sense of the main character of the main character.

Because we live in an age when heroes are few and far between, this kind of even-keeled approach to historical biography is all the more essential. We don't need any more fabulous hagiographies–unrealistic literary icons of unapproachable saints. And we don't need any more Freudian exposés–psychological analyses of debunked champions. Instead, we need honest portrayals of those men and women who have gone before us, who have marked out a pathway of faithfulness and valor through the extraordinary obstacles of ordinary life. We need real-life examples. We need to catch a glimpse of leadership in action.

Stephen Mansfield succeeds admirably at giving us this very kind of book. His prose style is vigorous, his historical sensibility is keen, and his clear-headed soberness is unswerving. He displays a very evident artist's touch–without neglecting either science or philosophy. Though his subject, the valiant virtue of Winston Churchill, might tend to loom larger than life in the hands of a lesser writer, he manages to stay firmly planted on *terra firma*. The result is an inspiring account of a very great man's legacy of leadership. But it is simultaneously an intimate account of a very normal man's persistence in principle.

There is a kind of romance manifest in these pages. But it is that unsentimental sort of romance that is the peculiar fruit of wisdom: a full appreciation of what is without the imaginative gloss of what isn't. It is therefore with great pleasure that I introduce this book–the first in a series of short biographical profiles of notable leaders–as both a passionate example of the artist's vision and an edifying example of the academician's understanding.

Stephen Mansfield has given us a heady dose of encouragement precisely because he has fully realized in the life of Churchill the fact that leadership is a vocation best nurtured on the medicine of mundanity and the potion of providence. And he has done it with all the zest and adventurousness of a novelist. For that we can all be thankful.

ACKNOWLEDGMENTS

It was my mother who first planted the seeds of historical awareness in my life. As our little military family moved from assignment to assignment in a green and brown Country Squire station wagon, she made sure that all twenty-some volumes of our encyclopedia rode with us. She read to us about the places we passed or the names on the statues we saw, and I remember that my first glimpses of how time and generations unfold, of how the past is somehow lurking just beneath the present, entered my mind on the wings of her voice. Most of my "exciting adventures" grow out of her influence and I am thankful beyond words.

One of the greatest delights of my life is my budding relationship with George Grant. Not only have I found in him a mentor and comrade in arms, but also a dear friend whose kindness, humor, and encouragement have renewed me. I think I am beginning to understand how steel can sharpen steel and how a threefold cord cannot easily be broken.

My assistant, Jackie Lusk, has repeatedly gone far beyond the call of duty on this and many other projects. Her devotion, discipline, encouragement, and laughter transform whatever she touches and I am truly grateful for our partnership.

Special thanks to my "warriors"–Jackie Lusk, Dawn Ruff, Dabney Mann, and Sandra Elkins–who really understand their contribution to my life better than I do. My deep appreciation also to Mary Venable and Shan White.

Others to whom I am indebted are Michael Peterson, who has paid more library fines for me than I will ever know about; Greg Webb, who stoked the Churchillian fires so many years ago; David Toberty, who has shared not only Churchill but life and destiny with me since those early days in "the Shak"; the MC's, whose lives are the laboratory for learning what I know about integrity and character; Thurston and Wilma Carter, who entrusted me both with their daughter and a unique opportunity to grow; and Don Finto, my pastor and friend, who daily models the kind of passion and character I thought had died out generations ago.

As dear as the friends and companions I have listed above are to me, my greatest and most heartfelt appreciation is for my family. My wife, Patricia, and our two children, Jonathan and Elizabeth, have sacrificed far more than they should have been asked to in recent years. Without a wife of such character or children of such delight I would never have had the heart or the freedom to do projects like this.

Soli Deo Gloria

INTRODUCTION

I often replay in my mind imaginary conversations with the great men and women of history. In these fanciful dialogues–which for some mysterious reason are set late at night in my favorite restaurant–I find myself eventually winding around to the appropriate moment for asking, "What is it that made you great?" Echoing back in my imagination are answers far from those I would expect, for I do not hear my companions reply "I was a great King," or "I was the unsurpassed genius of my age," or "I was a skillful leader in the decisive events of my day." Instead, I hear them answer with gentle determination, "I believed in certain eternal principles," or "I had, through suffering and difficulty, acquired a level of character that enabled me to shape my generation," or "I saw the problems of my day from a unique perspective which I knew could help solve them." It is greatness viewed in this light, imaginary or not, which is the only justification for this book, yet another study on the life of Winston Churchill.

One would think that Churchill's life had been by now thoroughly examined from every possible perspective. The painstaking labors of Martin Gilbert, Churchill's official biographer, have alone produced volumes of biography, official papers, and parallel lives. In addition, the recent work of William Manchester in *The Last Lion*, of Norman Rose in his *Churchill: An Unruly Life*, and even of critics like John Charmley in *Churchill: The End of Glory* have each added exhaustive research and invaluable insight to the already solid canon of Churchill studies.

What is intended here, though, is not at all the comprehensive analysis provided by these esteemed authors, but rather an attempt to answer the question, "What has Churchill to say to a new generation of leaders?" In other words, in view of all the wonderful literature on Churchill's life–the psychological treatises, the political investigations, the adoring reminiscences–how are we to understand him so as to attempt in our own time what might be called a "Churchillian brand of leadership."

This is not too much to ask, particularly when we consider the primary purpose of historical research throughout the centuries. For most of western history the study of the past was part of the field of moral philosophy. Men studied history primarily to discern the ways of Providence and acquire wisdom for their age. Far from the abstract, ivory tower approach so prevalent in our schools, the study of history was then considered eminently practical and men expected to live differently for the time they spent in the far off country of the past.

Certainly, on the matter of leadership Churchill has much to say to the present generation. His words, though, would undoubtedly cut across most current dogma and pop philosophy on the subject. For Churchill, leadership was more than what is revealed in academic transcripts, psychological test scores, or polished résumés. Books on dressing for success, guides to the "one-minute" add water and stir variety of leadership, and seminars that stress "image management" have no place in a Churchillian philosophy. Instead, for Churchill, leadership was primarily about eternal values, the civilizations they produce, and the individual character necessary to navigate the present in pursuit of a more glorious future. How very much we have to learn from Winston Churchill.

It would be a mistake, however, to try to extract Churchill's maxims of leadership from the fabric of his life. He was, perhaps above all else, an embodiment of the principles he revered and the civilization he sought to build. To understand the lessons of leadership Churchill has to teach, we must first understand the life Churchill had to lead and the fascinating manner in which his personal history reinforced his character of leadership. To visit once again, then, the life of Churchill as the most recent scholarship has presented it and afterward attempt to identify the primary pillars of Churchill's legacy will take us far in hearing the valuable counsel of a great man who "though dead yet speaks."

CHRONOLOGY OF WINSTON CHURCHILL'S LIFE

1874, November 30–Winston Churchill is born at Blenheim Palace.

1874, December–Mrs. Everest, Winston's nanny and primary spiritual influence, enters his life.

1874, December 27–He is baptized and his life dedicated to God.

1880, February 4–John Strange Spencer Churchill, Winston's brother, is born.

1888, April 17–He enters Harrow School.

1893, September–He enters the Royal Military College at Sandhurst.

1894, December–He graduates from Sandhurst.

1895, January 24–Lord Randolph Churchill, Winston's father, dies.

1895, April 1–He is commissioned as a lieutenant in the Fourth Queen's Own Hussars.

1895, July 3–Mrs. Everest dies.

1895, November–He first encounters armed conflict during a visit to Cuba.

1896, October 3–He arrives in India and begins his program of self-education.

1898, March 14–*The Story of the Malakand Field Force*, Winston's first book, is published.[1]

1898, September 2–In the Sudan, he takes part in the last cavalry charge in British history.

1899, September–He runs as a Conservative candidate for Oldham and is defeated.

1899, October 14–He sets sail for South Africa to cover hostilities for the *Morning Post.*

1899, November 6–Winston's *The River War*, which is highly critical of Lord Kitchener, is published.

1899, December 13–He escapes from prison in Pretoria, an adventure that makes him internationally famous.

1900, February 3–*Savrola*, his only novel, is published.

1900, October 1–He is elected as Conservative member of Parliament for Oldham.

1904, May 31–He joins the Liberal party.

1905, December 9–He becomes Under Secretary of State for the Colonies.

1906, January 2–His biography of his father, *Lord Randolph Churchill*, is published.

1908, April 24–He becomes president of the Board of Trade with Asquith's cabinet.

1908, September 12–He marries Clementine Hozier.

1909, July 11–Diana, the Churchill's first child, is born.[2]

1911, May 28–Randolph, the Churchill's second child and only son, is born.

1914, October 1–As First Lord of the Admiralty, he orders mobilization of the Royal Navy. Great Britain declares war on Germany three days later.

1914, October 7–Sarah, the Churchill's second daughter, is born.

1915, May 28–After the Dardanelles defeat he resigns as First Lord of the Admiralty.

1915, November 19–He takes command of the Grenadier Guards in France and later the Sixth Royal Scots Fusiliers.

1917, July 16–He assumes the role of Minister of Munitions.

1918, November 15–Marigold, the Churchill's third daughter, is born.

1919, January 15–He is made Secretary of State for War and Minister of Air.

1921, February 15–He is made Colonial Secretary and negotiates settlements in Ireland and the Middle East.

1921, June 29–Lady Randolph Churchill, his mother, dies.

1921, August 23–Marigold dies at the age of two.

1921, September 15–Mary, the Churchill's youngest child and fourth daughter, is born.

1922, October–He is defeated and put out of Parliament for the first time since 1910.

1922, November–The Churchills purchase Chartwell Manor.

1923, April 10–Volume I of *The World Crisis*, his history of World War I, is published.

1924, September–He switches to the Conservative party and is elected Member from Epping.

1924, November 7–Like his father before him, he becomes Chancellor of the Exchequer.

1930, October 20–His biographical *My Early Life* is published.

1933, October 6–The first volume of *Marlborough: His Life and Times* appears in print.

1939, September 3–He becomes First Lord of the Admiralty again as Britain declares war on Hitler's Germany.

1940, May 10–He becomes Prime Minister of England.

1940, May 13–He makes his famous "blood, toil, tears and sweat" speech.

1945, May 8–Victory in Europe Day celebrates the unconditional surrender of Germany.

1945, July 26–Bitterly defeated in a general election, he resigns as Prime Minister.

1946, March 5–In Fulton, Missouri, he delivers the famous "Iron Curtain" speech.

1948, June 2–The first volume of *The Second World War* is published in America.

1951, October 26–He becomes Prime Minister for the second time.

1953, December 10–Churchill is awarded the Nobel Prize in Literature.

1955, April 5–Becoming increasingly feeble, he resigns as Prime minister.

1956, April 23–The first volume of *History of the English-Speaking Peoples* is published.

1963, October 20–Diana, the Churchill's eldest daughter, takes her own life.

1965, January 24–He dies at home after a massive stroke.

WINSTON CHURCHILL:
THE CHARACTER OF LEADERSHIP

ℑℓ   ℑℓ   ℑℓ

*"What is the use of living, if it be not to strive
for noble causes and to make this muddled world
a better place to live in after we are gone?"*

*"People who are not prepared to do unpopular things
and to defy clamor are not fit to be Ministers
in times of stress."*

PROLOGUE

*I*t was January 30, 1965, a bone-chilling, overcast day fit for the passing of an age. Muffled intensity filled London's damp air. Along a route marked by sanded streets crowds gathered to twenty deep. Some of the eager spectators had spent the night where they stood, braving the bitter cold for the promise of a better view. Soon the long-awaited procession would be in sight and the strains of Handel's *Death March* would echo from the surrounding buildings. On the wheels of a gun carriage, never used before to honor a commoner, would pass the flag-draped remains of "the greatest Englishman." Sir Winston Leonard Spencer Churchill.

For three days Sir Winston's body had lain in state at Westminster Hall. More than 4,000 people an hour had passed by in hushed honor, the line of somber mourners stretching as far as three miles. Then the anticipated moment arrived and eight men of the Grenadier Guards gently carried the coffin out of the Hall to mount it on its gun carriage. Pulled by the Royal Navy gun crew, it then proceeded through Parliament Square and into Whitehall, around the Cenotaph, memorial to the British dead of two world wars, and past a large brick house where two lights burned. It was No. 10 Downing Street, the Prime Minister's residence. Sir Winston had lived there for almost a decade.

Before he died on January 24, he said he wanted his funeral "to have plenty of bands and soldiers." In honor of his request, more than 3,500 members of the military lined the parade route, many snapping to rigid "present arms" as the procession neared. Slowly, the coffin moved past the Admiralty, a drab building with two stone sea horses guarding the entrance. Sir Winston served there as First Lord in each of two world wars. Curving through Trafalgar Square, the procession snaked past the 145-foot column of Nelson and past the Canada House, Uganda House, South Africa House and Malaysia House, each ringing with the echo of empire. Turning onto Fleet Street and then Ludgate Hill, the parade marched slowly, solemnly toward St. Paul's Cathedral. The Union Jack that covered Sir Winston was a splash of color against the general dreariness.

Halting before the triumphant dome of St. Paul's, the Grenadier Guards, each more than 6 feet and 2 inches tall, hoisted their burden aloft and moved with measured steps into the Cathedral. The coffin appeared to float down the center aisle of the great Cathedral, passing the tombs of Wellington and "Chinese Gordon." As though in welcome the organ sounded the swells of *The Battle Hymn of the Republic* and the choir intoned, "He has sounded forth the trumpet that shall never sound retreat."

When the service ended, the coffin advanced toward the Thames to the wail of bagpipes. Passing Tower Hill, Sir Winston was carried onto the *Havengore* as the Royal Marine Band played *Rule Britannia.* The small boat moved steadily upstream and on both sides of the Thames the dock cranes lowered in honor of the man who visited there so faithfully during the days of the bombs. Lightning jets soared overhead; old men remembered through their tears and young men stared in wonderment.

On the BBC, President Eisenhower, speaking from St. Paul's, offered words of comfort: "Upon the mighty Thames, a great avenue of history, move at this moment to their final resting place the mortal remains of Sir Winston Churchill. He was a great maker of history, but his work done, the record closed, we can almost hear him, with the poet, say:

> *'Sunset and evening star,*
> *And one clear call for me!*
> *And may there be no moaning of the bar*
> *When I put out to sea...*
> *Twilight and evening bell,*
> *And after the dark!*
> *And may there be no sadness of farewell,*
> *When I embark...'"*

The body was taken at Festival Pier for the two hour rail journey to Hanborough Station. Driven then to Oxfordshire, the streets and country lanes lined with a grateful people, Sir Winston was laid to rest in the village churchyard at Bladon beside his mother and father. Ironically, his father had died on the same date seventy years before.

Winston Churchill's final resting place was only a mile from Blenheim Palace, ancestral home of the Dukes of Marlborough. It had been the place of his birth some 90 years before. At the Palace there is today, as there was then, a column. It is the Victory Column celebrating John Churchill, the first Duke of Marlborough. Inscribed on the column is a tribute written by Viscount Bolingbroke at the request of the Duke's widow. It is hard to measure how truly the words speak of the Duke's life, but the description they provide of Winston Churchill's life is uncanny, written as they were nearly two centuries before his birth.

> *The Hero not only of his Nation, but of his Age:*
> *Whose Glory was equal in the Council and in*
>   *the Field;*
> *Who, by Wisdom, Justice, Candour, and Address,*
> *Reconcil'd various, and even opposite Interests;*
> *Acquired an Influence*
> *Which no Rank, no Authority can give,*
> *Nor any Force, but that of superior Virtue;*
> *Became the fixed important Center*
> *Which united, In one common Cause,*
> *The principal States of Europe;*
> *Who, by military Knowledge, and irresistible*
>   *Valour,*
> *In a long series of uninterrupted Triumphs,*
> *Broke the Power of France,*
> *When raised the highest, when exerted the most,*
> *Rescued the Empire from Desolation,*
> *Asserted and confirmed the Liberties of Europe.*

And so it was done, and the mourners of the world who had assembled for the departing—among whom were citizens of 110 nations, six monarchs, five presidents, and fifteen prime ministers—were free to return to their lives in the world Sir Winston had worked to build, to the future he had struggled so valiantly to preserve.

A Stage
Set for Heroes

*W*inston Churchill entered the world during one of the most breathless times of change and upheaval in history. To understand how sweeping this change was, remember that the American Civil War, which occurred less than a decade before Churchill's birth, was fought with rifles, sabers, cavalry charges, and cannon. That war ended in 1865. Less than fifty years later, in 1914, World War I began. Amazingly, this war was fought with tanks, airplanes, machine guns, mustard gas, telephones, trucks, and submarines. In half a century the world had changed a millennium.

But more was changing than technology. Man's thinking was changing as well. Ideas long cherished and dearly loved, were put on trial like never before. In the early 1800's, Ludwig Feuerbach had taught that God did not create man, but man created the idea of God because of his psychological need to believe in a God. Few took notice at first, but those who did made much of it. Karl Marx noticed it, and included the idea that "Religion is the opium of the people" in his materialist interpretation of history. Charles Darwin also noticed it, and assumed it was true when he published his *Origin of the Species by Means of Natural Selection*, which challenged every Christian assumption about the origin of the universe and the creation of man. And in Vienna, a Jewish scientist by the name of Sigmund Freud also noticed it and concluded that religion more often than not gives rise to mental illness because what men call sins are actually taboos arising from incest and cannibalism. It was strange, but then so were most of the new ideas circulating during that unusual era.

Among the nations, England was undergoing the greatest change of all. Britain was the birthplace of the industrial revolution and her trains, steamships, factories, and banks made her the "workshop of the world." London had become the greatest exporter on earth, the largest city in the world–indeed, the largest city the world had ever known–and the center of world finance. Mirroring her astounding prosperity, Britain's population had also dramatically increased. In the century before Churchill's birth, the population of England tripled and the citizenry of London jumped from two million to five. True, there were rising problems of poverty and immorality, and technology had yet to catch up with the demands of urban sprawl, making London an asphyxiating and maddening experience, but it was a great time to be alive–if you were British.

Queen Victoria was already in the thirty-seventh year of her reign when Churchill was born and her Britannic Majesty was "by the Grace of God of the United Kingdom of Great Britain and Ireland and of the British Dominions beyond the Seas, Queen, Defender of the Faith, Empress of India." The sun truly never set on the British Empire. England ruled one quarter of the world's land mass and more than a quarter of the world's population–three times the size of the Roman Empire.

To be British was to rule the world. Every schoolchild knew the stories of "Chinese Gordon," the Charge of the Light Brigade, and Horatio Nelson; every Briton had faith in the pound sterling and the Queen; and every patriot knew by heart the Imperial poetry of Rudyard Kipling and songs like *The Death of Nelson* and *Soldiers of the Queen.* It was a certified Golden Age, as every Englishman knew, and there was no end in sight to the glory and the dream.

But this kind of heady optimism is notoriously blind and for those born in the last third of the 1800's, as Churchill was, the challenges looming on the horizon would soon test every comfortable assumption of Empire and every fiber of personal faith and courage. Before the century was out, the Boer War would demonstrate the horrors of a new kind of warfare and World War I would drive the lesson home at a cost of nearly a generation of young men. The Old Order would meet its match in the new democracy, the new morality, the new technology, and the new politics. A bumptious teenager called the United States would become a player in the international game and sleepy colonies the world over would begin thinking about ideas like independence, liberty, and destiny. Violence and revolution would become commonplace in the new century, and the doctrines of socialism would forever transform the aristocratic art of governing.

All of this prepared the way for a new brand of leadership. No longer would world events be shaped by disinterested courtiers. No longer would time-honored tradition and pageantry alone unify nations and stir men to gallantry. The upheavals of the new century would make sure of it. Soon, men who survived the meat-grinders of World War I, who held to the old ethics of work and sacrifice, who distinguished between theories of relativity and philosophies of relativism, who had sufficient wisdom to know that the past is only discarded to the detriment of the future, and yet who allowed the winds of change to carry them aloft to that future–men such as these would be in desperate demand by the early decades of the new century.

When the time came, Winston Churchill was ready to be among them. He knew he was destined to play a decisive role in the history of his times. He was eager to stand shoulder to shoulder with the visionaries and men of power who would forge the new century. Yet, from the beginning something set Churchill apart from the other leaders of his time and few, including at times Churchill himself, really understood why. In fact, even his biographers have failed to see it clearly, though the difference is actually a simple one. The fact is that in an age of mounting skepticism, Winston Churchill was a man of faith, a man who lived in the light of a vision unfashionably rooted in Scripture and centered in a sovereign God. He was a Christian, a man who passionately believed in the existence of truth, the reality of God, the power of His Church, and the culture it produces. Indeed, Churchill had an almost romantic attachment to the ideal of Christendom. He saw himself as its knight. He saw the British Empire as its standard bearer. And he saw history as a conflict between Christendom and the forces of blackest paganism.

This is the moral compass Churchill brought to the troubled twentieth century. Other leaders of his time floated in a sea of relativity. They had no moral bearings. They could not find a sufficiently firm foundation from which to oppose Nazi Germany, for example, because they did not know who they were or what they really believed. For Churchill it was simple. Nazism was idolatrous paganism, Hitler was "this wicked man," the battle was against "sinister forces of evil" opposed by the power of "Christian nations," and the present generation was divinely chosen to sacrifice in its glorious cause. End

of story. What Churchill brought to the battles of the twentieth century was the moral compass and world view of the
twelfth century coupled with a twenty-first century realism. It
is this vision, this historic and Christian vision, that is the
often-ignored key to understanding both Churchill's power as
a leader and his enduring relevance for our own times.

THE DRAMA BEGINS

It is fitting that Winston Churchill was born at Blenheim Palace, the residence a grateful Queen Anne built for John Churchill, the first Duke of Marlborough. John, "who never fought a battle he did not win nor besieged a city he did not take," led British forces in the defeat of the French at Blenheim in Bavaria on August 13, 1704.[1] The Palace was a royal reward for the Duke and was named for the site of his famous victory. Later, an observer noted that when the Palace is "seen in certain lights, its honey-coloured stone gleams like El Dorado Gold, encouraging all viewers to dream the impossible dream."[2]

What better place, then, for Lord Randolph Churchill and Jennie Jerome Churchill to bring their first-born son into the world. Lord Randolph, one of the rising stars of Victorian politics, was the second son of the seventh Duke of Marlborough. A leading figure in the Salisbury government, he was the kind of man who was both an intimate friend of the Prince of Wales and yet a favorite of the crowds that gathered in Parliament's visitor's gallery. They called him "Cheeky Randy" because of his intelligence and razor wit. His walrus mustache and bulging eyes made him easily recognizable to the workmen who hailed him on the streets. Many believed he was the next Prime Minister, but time would tell that his own emotional instability and arrogance worked against him.

Jennie Jerome, everyone agreed, was a ravishing beauty. Her father was Leonard Jerome, a wealthy American businessman for whom the New York race track, Jerome Park, was named. While on a trip through Europe with her mother, Jennie happened to be at the Royal Yacht Squadron regatta at Cowes in August, 1873, where Randolph Churchill was also in attendance. Jennie was in the first blush of womanhood and captured the eye of every young man with her brunette, dark-skinned beauty. Writing years later, Lord D'Abernon captured her for history.

> *I have the clearest recollection of seeing her for the first time…She stood on one side to the left of the entrance. The Viceroy was on a dais at the farther end of the room surrounded by a brilliant staff, but eyes were not turned on him or on his consort, but on a dark, lithe figure, standing somewhat apart and appearing to be of another texture to those around her, radiant, translucent, intense. A diamond star in her hair, her favourite ornament–its lustre dimmed by the flashing glory of her eyes. More of the panther than of the woman in her look, but with a cultivated intelligence unknown to the jungle. Her courage not less great than that of her husband–fit mother for descendants of the great Duke. With all these attributes of brilliancy, such kindliness and high spirits that she was universally popular. Her desire to please, her*

delight in life, and the genuine wish that all
should share her joyous faith in it, made her the
centre of a devoted circle.[3]

Randolph was smitten with this strong-willed American and proposed marriage within days of their first meeting. Jennie accepted. Randolph wrote his father that his fiancée "is nice, as lovable, and amiable and charming in every way as she is beautiful, and by her education and bringing-up she is in every way qualified to fill any position." After the matter of a dowry was settled, the couple was married. In his biography of his father, Winston Churchill later described the event: "On April 15, 1874, the marriage was celebrated at the British Embassy in Paris and after a tour–not too prolonged–up the Continent, Lord Randolph returned in triumph with his bride to receive the dutiful laudations of the borough of Woodstock and enjoy the leafy glories of Blenheim in the spring."[4]

Seven and half months later, a son was born to the couple. The circumstances of the birth foreshadowed the manner of the child's life. It was Saturday evening, November 29, 1874. The annual St. Andrew's Ball was underway at Blenheim Palace hosted by the Duke and Duchess of Marlborough. The guests, attired in the latest of fashion, were whispering and gesturing in tones of hushed astonishment. Inconceivably, the Duke's daughter-in-law, the brash but magnificent Jennie Jerome, had dared to make her appearance in a loose fitting gown, dance card in hand. But she was seven months pregnant and it was simply not done. All eyes were upon her as she took to the dance floor, pirouetting with astonishing strength and grace.

It was as she gaily danced through the list of waiting gentlemen that the pains began. Earlier that week, on Tuesday, she had fallen while walking through a field with a hunting party. Earlier that day, she had taken what her husband called a "rather imprudent and rough drive in a pony carriage."[5] These incidents, combined with the carefree dancing of the evening, took their toll and the child, soon to be notorious for impatience, gave notice of an appearance. Frantically, guests and servants searched for a birthplace. They assisted the expectant mother in the direction of her bedroom, but she never made it. She fainted and was carried into a little room just off Blenheim's main hall, a room that once belonged to the Duke's chaplain. The pains of labor continued through the night and into the next day. Finally, a boy was born and he was, according to the father, "wonderfully pretty so everybody says dark eyes and hair and very healthy considering its prematureness."[6] Weeks after the boy was born, on December 27th, the infant was baptized in the palace chapel by the Duke's chaplain. The child was named Winston Leonard Spencer Churchill.

Childhood:
Lonely but Not Alone

*I*t would be nice to report that the Churchills shared a warmly intimate home life. Sadly, nothing could be further from the truth and this is one of the most important factors in Winston's early life and psychological make-up. Quite to the neglect of their son, Randolph and Jennie Churchill gave themselves completely to their social ambitions. True, Victorian parents maintained an astonishing distance from their children, receiving them only at prearranged times and under the watchful eye of servants, but the Churchills were remote even by these standards. Of his mother, Winston later wrote, "I loved her, but at a distance." His father thought Winston was retarded, rarely talked to him, and regularly vented his mounting rage on the child. More than one historian has concluded that Lord Randolph simply loathed his son.

Fortunately, shortly after Winston was born he was given over to the care of his nanny, a Mrs. Elizabeth Anne Everest, and it is hard to overestimate her influence on him. She was everything the traditional image of the British nanny suggests:

plump, jolly, full of stories, and unceasingly overprotective. While his parents neglected him in pursuit of their social and political dreams, Mrs. Everest–or "Woom," as the boy called her–was the center of Winston's existence. Violet Asquith wrote that in Churchill's "solitary childhood and unhappy school days Mrs. Everest was his comforter, his strength and stay, his one source of unfailing human understanding. She was the fireside at which he dried his tears and warmed his heart. She was the night light by his bed. She was security." [7] She was also his first contact with genuine Christianity.

Mrs. Everest was a "low church" believer, meaning that she rejected "ornaments and ritual" and opposed all of the "popish trappings" in the Anglican church.[8] But she was also a passionate woman of prayer and she taught young Winston well. She helped him memorize his first Scriptures, knelt with him daily as he recited his prayers, and explained the world to him in simple but distinctly Christian terms. He, in turn, adored her and regarded her every word as on par with the law of God. Once while attending school in Brighton, he discovered that during worship services the students faced east when reciting the Apostles' Creed. Little Winston knew his nanny would not abide it. "I was sure Mrs. Everest would have considered this practice Popish and I conceived it my duty to testify against it. I therefore stood solidly to my front." Winston's devotion to his nanny on such a small issue is touching, but the more important lessons she taught him were also deeply embedded. Years later, when he was under fire on some remote battlefield or entangled in the most troubling difficulties, he found himself praying the prayers he had learned at Mrs. Everest's knee.

At the age of seven, Winston was sent away to St. George's School in Ascot; this marks the beginning of a dark and painful period in his life. At St. George's Winston encountered a sadistic schoolmaster by the name of Mr. Sneyd-Kynnersley who was notorious for his ritual "caning" of students who misbehaved. "Two or three times a month," Churchill remembered bitterly, "the whole school was marshaled in the Library, and one or more delinquents were haled off to an adjoining apartment by the two head boys, and there flogged until they bled freely, while the rest sat quaking, listening to their screams." [9] Since he was a strong-willed non-conformist who rarely chose the well-worn path, Winston often received Mr. Sneyd-Kynnersley's twenty lashes, which given his extremely sensitive skin must have been excruciating. In an explosion of pent-up anger, Winston once retaliated by kicking the headmaster's straw hat to pieces. Later he wrote, "My teachers saw me at once backward and precocious, reading books beyond my years and yet at the bottom of the Form. They were offended. They had large resources of compulsion at their disposal, but I was stubborn." [10] When Mrs. Everest undressed a vacationing Winston and discovered his back and bottom crisscrossed with welts, she summoned the child's mother who immediately removed him from the school, thus rescuing him from his ordeal.

Winston was then enrolled in a school run by two maiden sisters in Brighton. Unfortunately, the change in school brought no change in his attitude toward discipline. One teacher observed that he was "a small, red-haired pupil, the naughtiest boy in the class; I used to think he was the naughtiest small boy in the world." [11] Nevertheless, the two sisters treated Winston with kindness and slowly he began to respond. He recalled that "At this school I was allowed to learn things which interested me: French, History, lots of Poetry by heart, and above all Riding and Swimming. The impression of those years makes a pleasant picture in my mind, in strong contrast to my earlier schoolday memories." [12]

HARROW AND SANDHURST

⁋n 1888, Churchill entered prestigious Harrow School, then in its third century of training England's youth. At Harrow, young Winston passed some of the most formative years of his life, though it was a miracle that he was ever admitted in the first place. To get into the school he was required to take an examination in Latin, yet when the time came Winston could not answer a single question. He ended up putting an "I" on a piece of paper, then putting brackets around it, and then staring at it for an additional two hours. The paper, adorned also by several ink smudges, was then turned in to the Headmaster, a Dr. Weldon, who, miraculously, decided to let the boy pass. "It was from these slender indications of scholarship," Churchill later wrote, "that Dr. Weldon drew the conclusion that I was worthy to pass into Harrow. It is very much to his credit. It showed that he was a man capable of looking beneath the surface of things." [13]

The truth is that Churchill was the school dunce and that he never passed out of the "lower form." Initially, there were two students beneath him in rank. Those two soon dropped out, leaving Churchill at the bottom. When the students marched in rank across campus or into ceremonies, onlookers would cry out, "Isn't that Lord Randolph's son? Why, he is last of all!" [14] Young Winston never did improve much, but the one advantage of being in the lower form was that only English was studied there. "As I remained in the Third Fourth three times as long as anyone else, I had three times as much of it. I learned it thoroughly. Thus I got into my bones the essential structure of the ordinary British sentence–which is a noble thing." [15]

Winston not only suffered from poor academic standing at Harrow, but also from his small physical stature. He was tiny for his age, weak of limb, small and raspy in the chest, and he fell ill more than most boys. To compensate, he took up swimming and fencing, and he took to bullying a bit. On one occasion he sneaked up behind a boy approximately his size and pushed him into the swimming pool. The other boys warned Churchill that he had just aroused the ire of Leo Amery, a Sixth Former. Realizing his error, Winston apologized: "I am very sorry. I mistook you for a Fourth Form boy. You are so small." This proving unsatisfactory, he continued, "My father, who is a great man, is also small." At this, the older boy laughingly commended Churchill's "cheek" and let the matter end, much to Winston's delight. So it was that Churchill met Leo Amery, future Member of Parliament and formidable Tory politician.

At some point in Winston's younger days it was decided that a career in the Army suited him. He later remembered that the moment of decision came when his father visited him in his bedroom. Winston possessed a huge collection of toy soldiers, which he arranged in historically accurate positions all throughout his room. When his father arrived for a "formal visit of inspection,"…"he spent twenty minutes studying the scene–which was really impressive–with a keen eye and captivating smile. At the end he asked me if I would like to go into the Army. I thought it would be splendid to command an Army, so I said 'Yes' at once: and immediately I was taken at my word." The memory ought to have been a happy one for Winston, but the thrill left when he was eventually told of his father's motive: "For years I thought my father with his experience and flair had discerned in me the qualities of military genius. But I was told later that he had only come to the conclusion that I was not clever enough to go to the Bar." [16] Such was the tenor of Winston's crushing relationship with his father.

In 1892, after taking the entrance examinations three times and passing only by as large a miracle as the one needed to enter Harrow, Churchill entered Sandhurst, the British West Point. It meant a fresh start for him. All of his deficiencies in subjects like Latin and Mathematics ("that dismal bog") were left behind in deference to new, more stimulating topics like Tactics, Fortification, Topography, Military Law, and Military Administration. Winston loved the military life, with its sense of tradition and pageantry, and through it he became particularly fond of horses. Though he complained that he was cursed "with so feeble a body," he nevertheless forced himself to overcome–often by spending eight hours a day in the saddle–and finally graduated from the school in 1894, 8th out of a class of 150.

CUTTING THE TIES OF YOUTH

In the next year, 1895, three significant events occurred in Winston's life. First, he was commissioned as a lieutenant and joined the Fourth Hussars at Aldershot. "I passed out of Sandhurst into the world," he wrote. "It opened like Aladdin's Cave. From beginning of 1895 down to the present time of writing I have never had time to turn round. All the days were good and each day better than the other. Ups and downs, risks and journeys, but always the sense of motion, and the illusion of hope." [17] During his unusual career he served in nine different British regiments–the Fourth Hussars, the Thirty-first Punjab Infantry, the Twenty-first Lancers, the South African Light Horse, the Oxfordshire Hussars, the Oxfordshire Yeomanry, the Grenadier Guards, the Royal Scots Fusiliers, and the Oxfordshire Artillery.

It was also in 1895 that Lord Randolph died. For quite some time, he had been suffering the degenerative effects of a disease that some historians believe was syphilis. In the final months the disease had attacked his nervous system with horrible results: he became "subject to unexpected attacks, facial tremors, tremors of the lip and tongue, abrupt changes in the pupils of his eyes, impaired vision, splitting headaches, lapses of memory, delusions, depressions and dementia."[18] No one told Winston about his father's disease or its symptoms and he was therefore unable to mentally cushion his father's wounding attacks against him in the final months. Finally, at 6:15 on the morning of January 24th, Lord Randolph's ghastly ordeal ended and he slipped into eternity. Four days later, he was buried in the church yard at Bladon.

Churchill's own account of his father's death in *My Early Life* is typical of the forgiving devotion he felt for Lord Randolph: "My father died on January 24 in the early morning. Summoned from a neighbouring house where I was sleeping, I ran in the darkness across Grosvenor Square, then lapped in snow. His end was quite painless. Indeed he had long been in stupor. All my dreams of comradeship with him, of entering Parliament at his side and in his support, were ended. There remained for me only to pursue his aims and vindicate his memory. I was now in the main the master of my fortunes."[19]

That same year, Winston's aged nanny, Mrs. Everest, also died. The two had maintained a tender correspondence throughout his school years, even after she left the Churchill's employ. In the hot summer months of 1895 she lay suffering with peritonitis. Her sister wrote to Winston that Mrs. Everest was not well. He hurried to her side through a heavy rain shower only to find that she was more concerned about his wet jacket than about her own condition. He sat with her but soon had to return to Aldershot. While there he received another telegram warning that Woom's end was near. He fetched a doctor and again hurried to her side. She recognized him briefly when he arrived but soon after sank into a coma. Winston remained by her side, tenderly holding her hand until she died at 2:15 the following morning. "Death came very easily to her," he wrote later, "She had lived such an innocent and loving life of service to others and held such a simple faith, that she had no fears at all, and did not seem to mind very much."[20]

He was not done tending to her, though. He organized the funeral and contacted the other families she had served. Knowing how dearly his brother had loved Mrs. Everest, Winston took the time to go to his school to inform him of her death. Returning then, the two brothers purchased a wreath in the family name and paid for a headstone. At the funeral, he was surprised by the number of mourners and also by how deep his own mourning was. "I feel very low," he wrote his mother, "and find that I never realized how much poor old Woom was to me."[21] His lasting devotion to her is evidenced by the picture of her that sat on his desk throughout his life and lay at his bedside when his own death came seventy years later.

THE ANVIL OF INDIA

The ties of youth now largely cut, Lieutenant Churchill was ready to test himself in battle. Unfortunately, there were few opportunities: "I searched the world for some scene of adventure or excitement," he wrote. He decided that the rebellion in Cuba provided just the exposure to "real action" that he needed, so he took a leave of absence from the Army, signed on with *The Daily Graphic* as a journalist, and left for Cuba. On the eve of his twenty-first birthday, he came under hostile fire for the first time: "On this day when we halted for breakfast every man sat by his horse and ate what he had in his pocket. I had been provided with half a skinny chicken. I was engaged in gnawing the drumstick when suddenly, close at hand, almost in our faces it seemed, a ragged volley rang out from the edge of the forest. So at any rate I had been under fire. That was something!"[22]

Upon returning to Britain, he learned that his regiment had been ordered to India and that he was to garrison at Bangalore. India was an important transition for Churchill for reasons he could not have foreseen. Here, for the first time, he came into intimate contact with men of his own age who possessed a university education. He marveled at their breadth of knowledge and their ease of discourse on most any subject made him realize how narrow his own education had been. When it came to history, philosophy, law or theology, there were huge gaps in his understanding. In an explosion of curiosity and ambition, he began to devour books on his weakest subjects. With his mother shipping him books as fast as she could, he gorged himself on some of the greatest literature in the English language. This eager pursuit of knowledge was a turning point in Churchill's life, and the character he displayed in striving against his own inadequacies undoubtedly marked the beginning of his manhood.

But with manhood came man-sized crises and Churchill's reading opened a Pandora's box of religious skepticism from which he might never have recovered himself. In the field of philosophy he was confronted for the first time by scholars who systematically destroyed everything he had been taught about religion. He became angry that so many "myths" had been foisted upon him as divine truth: "Of course if I had been at a University my difficulties might have been resolved by the eminent professors and divines who are gathered there. At any rate, they would have shown me equally convincing books putting the opposite point of view. As it was, I passed through a violent and aggressive anti-religious phase which, had it lasted, might easily have made me a nuisance. My poise was restored during the next few years by frequent contact with danger." [23] Before long Churchill's atheism was tested and found wanting when he faced the prospect of death during the South African War. Until then, though, he rode the tide of skepticism then washing so destructively through his age.

It was in India that he also renewed acquaintance with a family friend, General Sir Bindon Blood. Through Blood's influence, Churchill joined the Malakand Field Force on the

Northwest Frontier of India and became involved in combat against Pathan tribesmen. Here he experienced not only the blistering heat of India, but the death of comrades in arms, the gut-wrenching fear of real battle, and the manly comfort, of loyal friends. These experiences built a muscular ruggedness in him and he soon gained a reputation for exceptional physical courage. This newfound boldness, joined with his sensitive and moody nature, made him something of a mystery to those who fought beside him. A contemporary described him as "a slight, red-headed, freckled snub-nosed young subaltern, vehement, moody, quickly responsive, easily hurt, taciturn at times and at times quite opinionative with a tumbling flow of argument, confident to the point of complacency, but capable of generous self-sacrifice, proud but no snob." [24]

THE PEN AND THE SWORD

This unique personality, combining as it did the manner of a soldier with the heart of a poet, led to the writing of *The Story of the Malakand Field Force*, Churchill's first book. Its style is like the fire of an automatic weapon: short bursts of highly charged words packaged in a crisp, authoritative narrative. The book met with wide popular success and was followed several years later by Churchill's only novel, *Savrola, A Tale of the Revolution in Laurania*. *Savrola* is what might be called autobiographical fiction, since it offers important insights into Churchill's character and even approaches predicting events in his life. "Would you rise in the world?" the hero asks, "You must work while others amuse themselves. Are you desirous of a reputation for courage? You must risk your life. Would you be strong morally or physically? You must resist temptations. All this is paying in advance; that is prospective finance. Observe the other side of the picture; the bad things are paid for afterward!" Though historians find more of the real Churchill depicted in *Savrola* than in most of his other works, he was embarrassed by the book: "I have consistently urged friends not to read it."

Churchill's battle experience in India only made him hungry for more and when he received word that Lord Kitchener was leading a force up the Nile into the Sudan, he was beside himself. Attempting to win an assignment to the campaign through his many influential friends, he found that he was blocked by the great Kitchener himself, still smarting from the criticisms of him that had appeared in Churchill's newspaper dispatches. Finally, the War office assigned Churchill to the 21st Lancers, making it possible for him to take part in the last cavalry charge in British history. It was a ghastly affair, and of the aftermath he wrote, "from the direction of the enemy there came a succession of grisly apparitions; horses spouting blood, struggling on three legs, men staggering on foot, men bleeding from terrible wounds, fish-hook spears stuck right through them, arms and faces cut to pieces, bowels protruding, men gasping, crying, collapsing, expiring." In his book, *The River War*, Churchill not only told the tale of the battle, but also took Lord Kitchener to task for his role in the desecration of a religious leader's tomb. It did not endear him to the British high command.

Following his adventures in the Sudan, Churchill realized that writing was a far better source of income than the Army and considered going to Oxford to earn that much-vaunted university education. Ever in pursuit of new adventure, he opted instead for a short stint in India. In 1899, he resigned his commission and decided to enter politics. He applied to the Conservative party for a Commons seat to contest and was given a dreary Manchester industrial suburb called Oldham. He was soundly defeated but not disheartened, and later wrote, "Live and learn! I think I might say without conceit that I was in those days a pretty good candidate. However, when the votes were counted, we were well beaten." As is always the case following failed political campaigns, pundits sought to place the blame: "Everyone threw the blame on me. I have noticed that they nearly always do. I suppose it is because they think I shall be able to bear it best."[25]

THE SOUTH AFRICAN WAR

⟨In 1899, a series of unfortunate events led the Transvaal Boers in South Africa to issue an ultimatum of withdrawal to the British. London ignored the ultimatum and war became inevitable. "The Boer ultimatum had not ticked out on the tape machines for an hour before Oliver Borthwick came to offer me an appointment as principal War Correspondent of the *Morning Post*," Churchill wrote. Without hesitation he accepted and soon found himself en route to South Africa. South Africa would prove to be a major turning point in Churchill's life and career, but not for reasons he could have anticipated. Shortly after arriving, a troop train that Churchill was on came under Boer attack and was derailed. Though his quick thinking and gift of command saved many lives, Churchill was captured by the Boers and taken to a POW camp in Pretoria. He found the experience humiliating and angrily determined to escape despite orders forbidding it. As he told a commanding officer, "I must escape. I am almost twenty-five years-old." Four weeks later, he was gone.

The tale of his escape is filled with the near miraculous. Churchill and two fellow captives had decided to slip out of the prison through a latrine window under cover of night. Their chances of success were slim but they were determined. When the agreed-upon hour arrived, the three donned Boer clothing and entered the latrine to await a rotation of the guards. The opportunity presented itself and Winston slipped through the open window to wait for the others in the bushes below. He waited in vain, though, because suspicious guards prevented his companions from joining him. Finally, after deciding to ignore the whispered urging of his friends to climb back into the building, Churchill merely stepped from the bushes, "strode into the middle of the garden, walked past the windows of the house without any attempt at conceal- ment, and so went through the gate. I passed the sentry at less than five yards." Churchill was free but far from peril. The compass and map he had planned to use were inside the prison with his friends. Armed only with seventy-four pounds sterling, four slabs of chocolate, and a few biscuits, he faced three hundred miles of hostile territory populated by people whose language he did not understand. Beyond that, within days his description and news of the reward for his capture would be known throughout the country.

After roaming for a while through Pretoria like any other Boer farmer, he discovered a train track and followed it to a nearby station. Within minutes a train arrived and when it began to roll out of the station Churchill waited for the engine to pass before hurling himself into one of the cars. He spent a restful night burrowed in empty coal sacks but awoke in time to jump from the train before daybreak. After finding water he settled into a ravine to await the next train that might take him west to friendly territory. He sat for hours, but no train arrived. Finally, in desperation, he began to walk the tracks only to discover that every bridge was manned by Boer guards. He discovered, too, that he had drawn the attention of "a gigantic vulture, who manifested an extravagant interest in my condition, and made hideous and ominous gurglings from time to time." [26]

He grew desperate and confused. For a while he sat "completely baffled, destitute of any idea what to do or where to turn." [27] Finally, he determined to walk toward some lights he saw in the distance, believing they must be the campfires of a Bantu tribe. As he neared, he discovered that the lights belonged instead to a mining settlement. He hesitated, but decided to seek help at one of the houses in the small township. When he knocked on the door he was met by a gruff man who aimed a menacing pistol in his direction. Churchill tried to bluff but taking note of the man's incredulity, he decided to tell the truth. After a long pause, the man lowered the pistol and exclaimed "Thank God you have come here! It is the only house for twenty miles where you would not have been handed over. But we are all British here, and we will see you through." [28] Churchill later said that at that moment he "felt like a drowning man pulled out of the water and informed he has won the Derby!" [29] With the help of his new companions, Churchill was hidden in a mine, then loaded onto a westbound train, and carried to the safety of neutral Portuguese East Africa. He arrived days later in Durban to a hero's welcome and found that accounts of his escape had filled the pages of newspapers throughout the world.

Churchill's newfound fame would change his life completely, but during his time in South Africa, a more important inner change had occurred. Since India and his readings in religious rationalism, Churchill had been a religious skeptic at best and more probably a complete atheist. But as he wandered the South African *veld* in his escape from the Boers, he was confronted with the utter inadequacy of his world view: "I found no comfort in any of the philosophical ideas which some men parade in their hours of ease and strength and safety. They seemed only fair-weather friends. I realized with awful force that no exercise of my own feeble wit and strength could save me from my enemies, and that without the assistance of that High Power which interferes in the eternal sequence of causes and effects more often than we are always prone to admit, I could never succeed. I prayed long and earnestly for help and guidance. My prayer, as it seems to me, was swiftly and wonderfully answered."[30] This was a critical change for Churchill and in time his restored faith would work its way into the very fabric of his expanding world view.

PRINCIPLES AND POLITICS

$\mathcal{E}$ncouraged by his newfound fame, Churchill re-entered politics. The citizens of Oldham were now overjoyed with their famous young candidate, particularly when during one of his speeches the wife of the man who had helped him escape in South Africa was found to be in the audience. Churchill was elected in a landslide and his popularity was so widespread that he was able to ensure the election of other Conservative candidates. Before entering Parliament the following February, he decided to make a speaking tour of the United States. His subject was his experience in the South African war, and though the independence-loving Americans were largely on the side of the Boers, Churchill quickly learned to play to both causes, making the tour a huge success. During his travels in the states Churchill also met Mark Twain. The famous author took his young guest to task for the British treatment of the Boers, but still kindly presented him with a signed set of his works and introduced him to a New York audience as "the hero of five wars, the author of six books, and the future Prime Minister of Great Britain."[31]

Back in England, Churchill found that there was a good deal of stir about the new young M.P. from Oldham when Parliament opened. A fellow M.P. said that "Churchill had not been in the Commons for five minutes until he was seen to lean back, tip his top hat over his forehead, cross his legs, bury his hands in his pockets and survey the scene as if he were the oldest, not the youngest member."[32] New members were not supposed to speak until they had been in the House for a month. Within four days Churchill was already trying to draw the Speaker's attention for permission to make a speech.

This early non-conformity should have signaled to everyone that Churchill could never be a loyal party member and, true to form, within months he began to distance himself from the Conservatives. Seeing himself only as a loyal servant of the crown, the champion of a British legacy horribly tarnished in the Boer War, party loyalty for him would always stand a distant second to his vision for the nation. Finally, in a dramatic scene on May 31, 1903, Churchill entered the House of Commons, looked briefly in the direction of the Conservative bench, bowed to the Speaker, and "crossed the floor" to the Liberal Party. The House erupted, but in 1905, when the Liberals swept into power, Churchill was rewarded with an appointment as the Under Secretary for the Colonies. He was thirty years old. Two years later, he was made a Privy Councilor.

Churchill's political life grew increasingly tumultuous. He ran as a Liberal in Manchester Northwest and won, was driven out by suffragettes, bounced back by winning a seat in Dundee, and was appointed President of the Board of Trade, Home Secretary, and First Lord of the Admiralty. Somewhere along the way he got married. The Countess of Airlie, who helped Churchill in his Dundee campaign, had a granddaughter who was a known beauty. Her name was Clementine Hozier and at twenty-three she was at the height of her splendor. Violet Asquith wrote that Clementine had a "face of classical perfection" and a profile like "the prow of a Greek ship."[33] Churchill was taken with her, though his rude staring almost put her off, and asked her to marry him during a visit at Blenheim. On September 12, 1908, the couple married at St. Margaret's in Westminster with the King of England and numerous high officials in attendance.

WORLD WAR I: THE DARDANELLES DISASTER

On August 4, 1914, negotiations between England and Germany broke down, signaling the beginning of World War I. Churchill was then First Lord of the Admiralty and had already seen the trouble coming. He was the visionary behind the Navy's dramatic modernization and behind the fleet having been sent to war stations long before hostilities were even announced. His efforts made him a hero throughout England and in the August 1914 edition of *Everyman*, a character sketch painted him in tones of honor.

> *Those who have worked with him declare that
> there never was a Minister of the Crown so
> eager and swift in his work; and if they find
> fault in him as a worker it is that he is apt to
> forget that all men are not endowed with his
> high talents and amazing energy. In times of
> relaxation he is never idle, and in times of great
> pressure he spares neither himself nor those
> around him, but he has the supreme gift of
> making his assistants in all ranks give the best*

of their labour freely to the task of the moment.
Rumour tells us that he is heartless in his
ambition and careless of every interest but his
own. To that description his own closest associ-
ates, political, official, and personal, give the lie;
and they will tell you that he is at once the
most exacting and the most generous chief
whom they have ever served.[34]

Such high praise was to be short lived, though. Churchill
was about to go through one of the most difficult crises of his
political career and the reason would be a strategy some considered the best tactical idea of the entire war. Armed with
insight from his extensive study of history, Churchill proposed
that to relieve pressure on the main ground fronts of the war,
the British Navy should attack the Central Powers at the flank.
The site chosen was the Dardanelles, the point at which
Europe and the Middle East join near Istanbul and the Aegean
Sea. Churchill believed that a naval attack there would support Russia in her struggles and squeeze Austria-Hungary and
Germany between two fronts.

The plan was good but the execution was a disaster.
Premature naval bombardments only served to warn the Turks
of invasion and repeated delays gave them time to reinforce
and entrench. British Admirals squabbled, hesitated, and demanded that the army clear the Turkish guns from the commanding cliffs. Weeks were lost to cowardly deliberation. When
the army did land, incompetence and confusion ruled. Naviga-
tional errors placed men miles away from their destination.
Generals who were fortunate enough to disembark at nearly
undefended beaches routinely made camp rather than charge
to the interior. Before long a bloody, foolish, macabre drama
began, with troops going "over the top" by the thousands only

to be cut down by entrenched Turkish machine gunners who could see them advancing hundreds of yards away. Churchill was beside himself as he watched his ingenious strategy collapse under the weight of military incompetence. He knew the plan was sound and yearned to be at the front to direct the assault himself. But from such a great distance he could only be tortured by the failure of his strategy, by mounting public rage, and by the death of more than 100,000 men.

What surely added to Churchill's torture was that had his counsel been heeded, the disaster in the Dardanelles might never have happened. In his recent book, *In Search of Churchill*, Martin Gilbert relates that Churchill was initially hesitant about the Dardanelles plan, responding to First Sea Lord Admiral Fisher's eager appeals, "I would not grudge 100,000 men because of the great political effects in the Balkan peninsula: but Germany is the foe, and it is bad war to seek cheap victories and easier antagonists." [35] Eventually Churchill was won over to the plan by the enthusiastic endorsement of every member of Asquith's War Council.

Though he was willing to champion the strategy, Churchill thought he saw a flaw in the decision to use naval forces alone without the support of troops. Lord Kitchener was emphatic that troops were unnecessary, that naval forces could easily win the day. Churchill remained unconvinced and specifically requested that the Cabinet Secretary record his dissent on the matter. A few days later, Churchill, still uneasy, decided to deploy the tiny Naval Air Service under his command when Lord Kitchener refused him the use of the Army's Flying Corps. Tragically, Lord Kitchener's belief that troops were unnecessary proved horribly wrong, and when they finally did land it was more than thirty days after the naval bombardment. They were butchered, by the thousands, and Churchill was blamed. [36]

Churchill knew he was a scapegoat and the betrayal cut deep. His prestige and power were fatally shattered. He was removed from the Admiralty and made Chancellor of the Duchy of Lancaster, a post he resigned within five months. It was a dark time of isolation and ridicule. "I'm finished," he told a friend, and when the friend protested, he asserted, "No, I'm done." Oddly, Churchill was scheduled to sit for the painting of a portrait during this bleak time. He kept the appointment, but as the painter William Orpen recorded, "All he did was sit in a chair before the fire with his head buried in his hands, uttering no word." [37] It was worse than anyone knew. Churchill took comfort in the "citadel of the heart," his family, but Clementine alone understood how wounded he really was: "The worst part of our life together was the failure of the Dardanelles expedition. Winston was filled with such a black depression that I felt that he would never recover from it, and even feared at one time that he might commit suicide." [38]

Despite this blow, the lure of a great conflict drew Churchill out of the darkness. Recovering himself, he took a Colonel's commission with the Grenadier Guards and was assigned to the Royal Scots Fusiliers in charge of a battalion. He was older now than when he had last seen the battlefront and he shared his more mature reflections on war and himself with Clementine: "So much effort, so many years of ceaseless fighting and worry, so much excitement and now this rough fierce life here under the hammer of Thor, makes my older mind turn for–the first time I think to other things than action . . . Sometimes also I think I would not mind stopping living very much. I am so devoured by egoism that I would like to have another soul in another world and meet you in another setting...But I am not going to give in or tire at all. I am going on fighting to the very end in any situation open to me from which I can most effectively drive on this war to victory." [39]

In the meantime, Churchill's friend and fellow Liberal, Lloyd George, managed to bring down the Asquith Government in December of 1916. Churchill was still too associated with the Dardanelles affair to invite into the Cabinet, but the new Prime Minister did appoint him Minister of Munitions in July of 1917. This was the perfect outlet for Churchill and through his skillful management, and particularly his control of the nitrate trade, he ensured that everything England needed was available in abundance until war's end. Lloyd George and Churchill made an effective team and on November 11, 1918, Armistice Day, the two quietly celebrated victory during dinner at Downing Street: "We were alone in the large room from whose walls the portraits of Pitt and Fox, of Nelson and Wellington, and–perhaps somewhat incongruously–of Washington then looked down. My own mood was divided between anxiety for the future and desire to help the fallen foe. From outside the songs and cheers of the multitudes could be remotely heard like the surf on the shore." [40]

THE AGE OF POLITICAL TURMOIL

With the conclusion of the War, Churchill became Secretary for War. His thankless task was to manage the transition of thousands of soldiers back into civilian life, a job he energetically completed with speed and efficiency. But in 1922, Lloyd George's government was toppled by Conservatives under Bonar Law and Churchill found himself without a seat in the Commons. He ran in the Leicester West Division but lost. He ran for a seat in the Abbey Division of Westminster and lost by forty-three of the 22,778 votes cast. Finally, he ran for a seat in the Epping Division of Essex as a Constitutionalist and won in a Conservative Party sweep. Soon afterward, Prime Minister Baldwin shocked Churchill by inviting him to become the Chancellor of the Exchequer, a position his father, Lord Randolph, once had held. Churchill, moved to be walking in his father's footsteps, eagerly agreed to the position and soon donned the same robes of office worn by his father in 1896.

The next several years were rocky for Churchill. With Baldwin's backing he returned England to the gold standard which threw the British economy into a tailspin and prompted the General Strike of 1926. Major industries suffered, unemployment skyrocketed and, once again, Churchill was blamed. The storm over the economy did not help to bolster Churchill's sagging relationship with Baldwin. Nor was he in agreement with Baldwin's pacifist sentiments about military threats on the continent.

In the election season of 1929, Baldwin gently wooed the country with the slogan "Safety First," but Churchill stormed against a Labor government he called the "Party of Plunder." On May 30th, as election returns poured in at Downing Street, Churchill exploded with rage as each new report confirmed a Labor landslide. Not only was he out of office, he was also branded an archaic reactionary because of his actions as Chancellor. Two years later, when Baldwin joined the tottering Ramsay MacDonald in a National government, Churchill was excluded from power, and so, "The night of May 30, 1929, at Downing Street was thus the beginning of a grim decade in which Churchill, although still in Parliament, would stay unheeded and alone in what he called the wilderness of politics."[41]

THE YEAR OF THE LOCUSTS

It is hard to exaggerate how despised and isolated Churchill was during these years. In Moscow, Stalin received a British delegation led by Lady Astor and inquired about Churchill. "Churchill?" Lady Astor replied, "Oh, he's finished." It was 1932. Politicians considered him an embarrassment, the British people had not forgotten the Dardanelles or Churchill's follies at the Treasury, and he was actually more popular in the United States than in his own country. Adding to his estrangement was his opposition to Indian independence. When Mahatma Gandhi visited England in 1931, Churchill simply refused to see him even though Gandhi was extolled by Anglican clergymen and had tea with the King and Queen. Churchill's intransigence on India merely enhanced his unfortunate dinosaur image.

During these painful years Churchill found solace at Chartwell, his beloved home in Kent. Here, with his wife and three children, he created a world free from the tormenting barbs of public life in which he could write, create, invest himself in the land, and celebrate with his friends. Needing the channel for his effusive energy that politics normally provided, he lost himself in a flurry of activity. With his own hands he excavated ponds, lakes, and a swimming pool, constructed waterfalls, built a tree house and a garden cottage for the children, put up walls, and raised animals. With dreams of becoming a gentleman farmer he purchased livestock and filled the estate with pets: marmalade cats, goldfish and golden orfe, ruddy sheldrakes, varieties of geese, black and white swans, and an infinite variety of dogs. The livestock proved an expensive failure, but the pets were among his greatest joys and he fed most of them with his own hand, calling each by name—even the fish.

Chartwell's guests were also a fascinating variety. On any given day, T. E. Lawrence might unexpectedly roar up the drive on a motorcycle wearing his Arabian robes. Charlie Chaplin might be found in heated debate with Churchill about socialism and its ills. There was also Professor Frederick Lindemann, the Oxford physicist. He had theoretically determined the reasons planes go into a spin and when military officials would not accept his research he learned how to fly, put his own plane into a spin, and successfully pulled it out again. Churchill loved him for his courage. Brendan Bracken was also a favorite. An M.P., financier, and newspaperman who was passionately loyal to Churchill, Bracken was probably his closest confidant during the wilderness years. Lord Max Beaverbrook was also a member of the Chartwell crew, admired by all for his agile mind and acid wit. "Some people take drugs," Churchill remarked, "I take Max."[42]

In addition to his friends and his home, Churchill also devoted himself to a staggering literary output. He published his autobiographical *My Early Life* in 1930, completed his history of World War I, *The World Crisis*, in 1931, published a collection of his writings called *Thoughts and Adventures* in 1932, and wrote the four thick volumes of his life of Marlborough, which he finished in 1938. In 1937, he finished his biographical essays, called *Great Contemporaries*, and though the work would not be finished until the 1950's, he did most of the writing on his *History of the English-Speaking Peoples*. Churchill's literary aspirations had been fueled by his trip to North America in 1929. He stayed at San Simeon as a guest of William Randolph Hearst, visited Civil War battlefields in anticipation of a book on the subject, and invested heavily in the New York Stock Market just before the crash. Churchill was at Wall Street to witness the chaos when a distraught stockbroker threw himself out of a skyscraper window.

During this troubling period of political isolation, Churchill's burden became heavier when he was called upon to support a friend in the face of overwhelming opposition and at great political cost to himself. In 1936, King Edward VIII ascended the throne upon the death of his father, George V. Not long afterward, Edward announced his intention to marry Mrs. Wallis Warfield Simpson, a divorced American. The Church of England, the Baldwin government, and the British people were all against the proposed marriage. Churchill's romantic attachment to the monarchy would not allow him to abandon his sovereign, though, and he worked tirelessly to change public opinion and slow the political machinery working against Edward. In spite of his efforts, Edward abdicated on December 10, 1936. Since it was Churchill who as Home Secretary had proclaimed Edward's title as Prince of Wales, he felt a special duty in the matter: "I should have been ashamed if, in my independent and unofficial position, I had not cast about for every lawful means, even the most forlorn, to keep him on the throne of his fathers." Churchill's support for Edward only distanced him further from the political and social mainstream, filling his wilderness years with even more ridicule and loneliness.

THE GATHERING STORM

The people of England soon found King Edward's abdication driven from their minds by a far greater threat to their civilization: Adolf Hitler. Following World War I, Germany was forced by the Treaty of Versailles to submit to humiliating disarmament and a harsh schedule of reparation payments. The result was a broken people and a spiraling economy. Adolf Hitler fed on the natural bitterness of the German people. Through his angry rhetoric and carefully orchestrated political rallies, Hitler turned the rage of the nation toward the Jews and launched a plan of rearmament in defiance of postwar agreements. His dream of a new age of Teutonic domination struck a responsive chord in the humiliated Germans who were soon willing to pay any price to reclaim their tarnished glory. Unfortunately, England's leaders, remembering the carnage of the "war to end all wars," convinced themselves that Hitler's grievances were justified and that his demands were reasonable. They were deceived, and their resultant failure to act soon permitted unparalleled death and destruction.

Churchill tried desperately to warn England about the "tumultuous insurgency of ferocity and war spirit raging in Nazi Germany." [43] As early as March of 1933, he told the House of Commons that "Nothing in life is eternal, but as surely as Germany acquires full military equality with her neighbors while her own grievances are unredressed and while she is in the temper which we have unhappily seen, so surely should we see ourselves within measurable distance of the renewal of general European war." [44] Sadly, his trumpet calls fell on deaf ears: "Although the House listened to me with close attention, I felt a sensation of despair. To be so entirely convinced and vindicated in a matter of life and death to one's country, and not be able to make Parliament and the nation heed the warning, or bow to the proof by taking action was an experience most painful." [45]

England's leaders excused Churchill as an alarmist and a saber-rattler. Clinging to their deception, they signed treaties with Hitler promising "peace in our time" and drew lines in the sand which they quietly drew again when Hitler ignored them. They made excuses when Germany annexed Austria, occupied the Sudetenland, and engulfed Czechoslovakia. Even when a Nazi-Soviet pact was concluded and Germany invaded Poland on September 1, 1939, Prime Minister Chamberlain and his Foreign Secretary, Lord Halifax, searched frantically for a compromise. Two days later, exhausted and overwhelmed by the course of events, Chamberlain announced that England and Germany were at war. But he needed the very man whose counsel he had ignored for so long, and so it was that Churchill–after almost a quarter of a century's absence–found himself once again First Lord of the Admiralty. When the Admiralty informed the fleet of its new chief, the signal was simply, "Winston is back!" The wilderness decade–"the years the locust had eaten"–was over.

WALKING WITH DESTINY

Churchill was not long at the Admiralty, though. On May 8, 1940, Leo Amery, once the boy young Winston dunked in the Harrow swimming pool, rose in the House of Commons, pointed his finger at Prime Minister Neville Chamberlain, and said, "You have sat here too long for any good you have been doing. Depart, I say, and let us have done with you. In the name of God, go!" The words were first uttered by Oliver Cromwell in dismissing the Long Parliament in 1653. In 1940, these same words expressed the frustration of a nation whose leaders did nothing while Adolf Hitler's Germany invaded the Netherlands, Belgium, and France. Two days later, Prime Minister Chamberlain resigned.

On the same evening, Churchill received a message from Buckingham Palace: "I was taken immediately to see the King. His majesty received me most graciously and bade me sit down. He looked at me searchingly and quizzically for some moments, and then said: 'I suppose you don't know why I have sent for you?' Adopting his mood, I replied: 'Sir, I simply couldn't imagine why.' He laughed and said: 'I want to ask you to form a Government.' I said I would certainly do so." [46] Thus,

at sixty-six years of age, Winston Churchill became Prime
Minister of England. He served from 1940 to the end of the
War in 1945, but never was he as magnificent as during his
first address to the House of Commons.

> *I would say to the House, as I said to those
> who have joined this Government: 'I have noth-
> ing to offer but blood, toil, tears and sweat.' We
> have before us an ordeal of the most grievous
> kind. We have before us many, many long
> months of struggle and of suffering. You ask,
> what is our policy? I will say: It is to wage war,
> by sea, land and air, with all our might and
> with all the strength God can give us: to wage
> war against a monstrous tyranny, never sur-
> passed in the dark, lamentable catalogue of
> human crime. That is our policy. You ask, What
> is our aim? I can answer in one word: Victory—
> victory at all costs, victory in spite of all terror,
> victory, however long and hard the road may
> be; for without victory, there is no survival. Let
> that be realized; no survival for the British
> Empire; no survival for all that the British
> Empire has stood for, no survival for the urge
> and impulse of the ages, that mankind will
> move forward towards its goals. But I take up
> my task with buoyancy and hope. I feel sure
> that our cause will not be suffered to fail
> among men. At this time I feel entitled to claim
> the aid of all, and I say, "Come, then, let us go
> forward together with our united strength."* [47]

Years later, when Clement Attlee was asked what Churchill did to win the war, he replied simply, "Talk about it." [48] Attlee was right. Churchill's weapons were his words; passionate words loaded with faith and vision. With them he defined the issues of the war and gave meaning to the horrible sacrifices victory demanded. Beyond his words, though, Churchill came to symbolize the same resolute opposition to tyranny he hoped to inspire. His "V for Victory" sign, his physical energy, his lifting sense of humor, and even his frequent tears made him on an international scale what he actually was: a romantic embodiment of faith in a destined future, of promised "sunlit uplands" awaiting mankind in its "upward journey."

Nothing tested all this quite like the reign of terror that Churchill called "The Battle of Britain." Following the near-disastrous Dunkirk evacuation early in the war, German bombs fell like rain on England, destroying much of London and killing nearly 50,000 Britons. England was weak, vulnerable, and alone against the possibility of Nazi invasion. Yet in that desperate hour, Churchill exploded into action with such force that he jolted the nation out of its numbing fear. He roared onto the radio, instilling courage and defiance in his suffering people. He rushed into the pummeled neighborhoods as soon as the air raids ended, always joking, weeping, challenging, and encouraging. The nation took comfort when Winston and Clementine calmly walked arm in arm amid the rubble in the streets and when the Prime Minister himself slept in a bunker as so many others were forced to do. Forgetting their myriad troubles for a moment, men cheered when their leader publicly insulted Adolf Hitler, refused the Führer's overtures of peace, or spoke of the future as though it was a certainty he could personally guarantee. Some have said that Churchill saved England during those terrible months, but if he did so it was because he came to symbolize everything men believed the British lion to be.

For Churchill, the primary issue of the war was faith. He firmly believed that World War II was a battle between Christendom and the sinister paganism of Adolf Hitler and throughout the War he replenished his unusual moral courage in worship and prayer. In August of 1941, Churchill met President Roosevelt at Placentia Bay, Newfoundland, for the meeting that would ultimately produce the Atlantic Charter. During a break in the Conference, the dignitaries gathered on the deck of the *Prince of Wales* for a worship service that for Churchill symbolized the whole nature of the war effort: "This service was felt by all of us to be a deeply moving expression of the unity of faith of our two peoples and none who took part in it will forget the spectacle presented that sunlit morning on the crowded quarter-deck: the symbolism of the Union Jack and the Stars and Stripes draped side by side on the pulpit; the American and British chaplains sharing in the reading of the prayers; the highest military and naval officers of Britain grouped in one body behind the President and me; the close-packed ranks of British and American sailors completely intermingled, sharing the same books and joining fervently together in the prayers and hymns familiar to both."[49]

What many remember most vividly of Churchill during the war years was his incredible energy and movement. It was as though his memories of the debacle in the Dardanelles made him vow he would never again be separated from the scene of action. He was everywhere during World War II. While Stalin and Roosevelt stayed largely at home, the Prime Minister of England drew enemy fire in Athens, rallied the troops in Northern Africa, strengthened the Alliance in Washington, and proposed conferences with leaders all over the world. Churchill believed he had to be at the center of action to be effective in command. He was hands on, involved, and eager to master the details. Often he won arguments about policy and tactics simply because he was in better command of the facts. He believed that he understood more clearly than others the course the war would take and how it could be won, but only because he had invested himself in mastering the cold realities of the problems his nation faced.

THE WILDERNESS AGAIN

Churchill's faith in all he fought for and in all he believed of the British people was severely tested when eighty days after the surrender of Germany, the British voters removed the seventy-one year-old leader from office. Churchill was stunned. When King George offered to honor him with the Order of the Garter, he bitterly declined by saying, "I could not accept the Order of the Garter from my Sovereign when I had received the order of the boot from his people."[50] The rejection hurt him deeply. He called Labor's victory at the polls "one of the greatest disasters that has smitten us in our long and checkered history."[51] He was sorely tempted to retire, but once he checked his emotions and began to weigh his options, he realized that he could never leave politics: "I have naturally considered very carefully what is my own duty in these times. It would be easy for me to retire gracefully in an odor of civic freedom, and this plan crossed my mind frequently some months ago. I feel now, however, that the situation is so serious and what may have to come so grave that I am resolved to go forward carrying the flag as long as I have the necessary strength and energy and have your confidence."[52]

Before long a new cause put fresh fire into Churchill's soul. As he had once prophesied the rise of Nazi Germany, he again donned the mantle of Old Testament prophet to warn the world of the growing threat of Communism. At the invitation of President Truman, Churchill made a speech at Westminster College in Fulton, Missouri, that became known as the "Iron Curtain Speech." In it he defined the issues of the Cold War and sounded the call to battle for the Western democracies. The speech was Churchill at his best; crisp, historical, passionate, and uncompromising.

> *From Stettin on the Baltic to Trieste in the Adriatic an iron curtain has descended across the Continent. Behind that line lie all the capitals of the ancient states of Central and Eastern Europe–Warsaw, Berlin, Prague, Vienna, Budapest, Belgrade, Bucharest and Sofia–all these famous cities and the populations around them lie in what I must call the Soviet sphere and are all subject in one form or another not only to Soviet influence but to a very high and in many cases increasing measure of control from Moscow.*[53]

> *Last time I saw it all coming and cried aloud to my own fellow countrymen and to the world, but no one paid any attention. Up until the year 1933 or even 1935 Germany might have been saved from the awful fate which has overtaken her and we might all have been spared the miseries Hitler let loose upon mankind. There never was a war in all history easier to prevent by timely action than the one which*

has just desolated such great areas of the globe.[54]

We are now confronted with something quite as wicked but in some ways more formidable than Hitler because Hitler had only the Herrenvolk pride and the anti-Semitic hatred to exploit. He had no fundamental theme. But these thirteen men in the Kremlin have their hierarchy and a church of Communist adepts, whose missionaries are in every country as a fifth column, obscure people, but awaiting the day when they hope to be absolute masters of their fellow countrymen and pay off old scores. They have their anti-God religion and their Communist doctrine of the absolute subjugation of the individual to the state, and behind this stands the largest army in the world in the hands of a government pursuing imperialist aggression as no Czar or Kaiser has ever done.[55]

The speech shook the uneasy and artificial peace that the Western world clung to so desperately in the wake of World War II. Leaders, particularly in the United States, tried to believe that Russia was, as Roosevelt had said, an "ideological power" like America, seeking only equality and prosperity for its people. The Soviet Union was an ally, after all, and Stalin was simply an astute power politician who wanted to preserve the territorial integrity of his nation. Once again, it fell to Churchill to proclaim the disturbing news to the world. Men might resent it and seek to silence him, but the cause of Christian civilization lay in the balance and he could not leave the challenge unanswered.

Upon returning to England after the speech, Churchill spared Prime Minister Attlee and his government no amount of grief. "When I am abroad," he said, "I always make it a rule never to criticize or attack the Government of my own country. I make up for lost time when I come home."[56] He loudly opposed Indian independence, devaluation of the pound, the socialist nature of Britain's economic policies, and, most of all, the almost complete blindness Attlee showed to "the Communist menace." In Parliament, tensions between Conservatives and Laborites mounted and in the election of 1950 Churchill almost made a comeback. Finally, in October of 1951, the Conservatives won enough seats to hold a majority in the House and on October 26, 1951, Churchill–one month from his seventy-seventh birthday–was invested by King George VI once again with the seal of office.

FINAL BATTLES

The role of Prime Minister felt familiar, but the world had changed considerably in his five years out of office. Tensions in India between Muslim and Hindu, the death of King George VI, the death of Stalin, the atomic arms race, and mounting economic problems at home all added to the burdens of office for the aging Churchill. Making matters worse, on June 10, 1953, he suffered a paralytic stroke that took him from his duties for several months. His loyal staff knew that he was never quite as sharp after the stroke and they secretly feared that the stress of office would lead to another more damaging attack. Finally, on April 5, 1955, following the advice of family and doctors, Churchill resigned.

The last decade of Churchill's life was filled with all the honors one might expect: the French Cross of Liberation, the American Freedom Award, and even honorary citizenship in the United States, received for him by his son in a Rose Garden ceremony at the White House. But it was also a time of sadness. Churchill had outlived most of his close friends, so many having lost their lives in the wars their generation was called upon to fight, and he found himself largely alone. His memories, as memories often are for the aged, were more vivid and inviting than the tedious existence he found himself living. He still enjoyed painting and visiting the homes of his wealthy international friends, but declining health brought on by strokes and several falls made travel an impossibility after the early 1960's. Of this stage in Churchill's life, scholars are fond of remembering the words he wrote about the death of the first Duke of Marlborough, who had "lingered on in surly decrepitude. How much better would it have been, had he been cut off in his brilliant prime." [57] Finally, in 1965, Churchill suffered a massive stroke and, after lying motionless in a coma for nine days, he died at eight o'clock in the morning on Sunday, January 24, 1965.

In the years before his death, Churchill's children lovingly expressed their feelings for their famous father and their tender words stand as a most eloquent benediction. "It is hardly in the nature of things," Mary wrote to her father, "that your descendants should inherit your genius–but I earnestly hope they may share in some way the qualities of your heart." Randolph, just a few years before his father's death, wrote, "Power must pass and vanish. Glory, which is achieved through a just exercise of power–which itself is accumulated by genius, toil, courage and self-sacrifice–alone remains. Your glory is enshrined forever on the unperishable plinth with the centuries." And just before his death, Mary assured her father that, "In addition to all the feelings a daughter has for a loving, generous father, I owe you what every Englishman, woman and child does–Liberty itself." [58]

up   *up*   *up*   *up*   *up*

Today, in Westminster Abbey, there is a marble tablet inscribed with a message for the ages. It calls mankind to think of duty, of character, and of greatness. It says simply,

"Remember Winston Churchill."

Winston Churchill:
The Pillars of Leadership

✧ ✧ ✧

"Come on now all you young men, all over the world. You have not an hour to lose. You must take your places in Life's fighting line. Don't be content with things as they are. Enter upon your inheritance, accept your responsibilities. Raise the glorious flags again, advance them upon the new enemies, who constantly gather upon the front of the human army, and have only to be assaulted to be overthrown. Don't take No for an answer. Never submit to failure. Do not be fobbed off with mere personal success or acceptance. You will make all kinds of mistakes; but as long as you are generous and true, and also fierce, you cannot hurt the world or even seriously distress her."

"Why is it the ship beats the waves when the waves are so many and the ship is one? The reason is that the ship has a purpose."

His Father

"Solitary trees, if they grow at all, grow strong; and a boy deprived of a father's care often develops, if he escapes the perils of youth, an independence and vigour of thought which may restore in after life the heavy loss of early days." [1]

In this age of the *Mommy Dearest*, what-bad-things-my-parents-did-to-me type of exposé, it is refreshing to hear someone declare that to be without a father, or at least a good one, is not necessarily to be condemned to a wounded existence or cursed with lifelong failure. On the contrary, there may even be in it the inspiration for greatness. Winston Churchill found this inspiration, but the price he paid for it was a tragic and heartbreaking relationship with his father.

Young Winston worshipped his father, the dashing and eloquent Lord Randolph Churchill, rising star of the Victorian Salisbury government. But in searching for the parental devotion and approval that ought to have been his, Winston collided with the steely arm of heartless rejection. His son, Randolph, later wrote that "the neglect and lack of interest in him shown by his parents were remarkable, even judged by the standards of late Victorian and Edwardian days."[2] In his entire life, he could boast of only three or four intimate conversations with his father. Abandoned to boarding schools during most of his youth, his letters home were filled with lonely pleas for his parents to visit and tender efforts to stir the affection of a father he knew mainly from newspaper articles. During this time it was not out of character for Lord Randolph to make a speech very near Winston's school, yet never cross the street to visit his son. He determined, he once mysteriously stated, to maintain before his son "a stony and acid silence."[3]

When Winston entered Sandhurst the situation grew no less heartrending. Of the few occasions he did accompany his father, Winston later wrote that Lord Randolph "froze me into stone" if any expressions of intimacy were attempted.[4] Such efforts were rare, though, for the young man's desperate craving for affection was held in check by the sheer dread his father inspired.

When a valuable watch, long in the Churchill family, fell into a stream near a deep pool at Sandhurst, Winston, fearing his father's wrath, instantly took off his clothes and plunged in to retrieve it. Failing to find it, he arranged to have the pool dredged. That proving fruitless, he paid twenty-three soldiers to dig a new course for the stream and then borrowed the school fire engine to pump the pool dry. He found the watch and sent it to a London watchmaker's shop for repair. Unfortunately, Lord Randolph discovered both the watch and its story. In the angry letter that followed, Winston was assured that his conduct was "shameful," that he was a "young stupid" who was "not to be trusted," and that his younger brother, Jack, was "vastly" his "superior." Winston, far from the adolescent who might have deserved such a tongue-lashing, was twenty years old at the time. Unbeknownst to Winston, Lord Randolph's grip on reality was even then loosening under the force of his terminal disease and, tragically, their relationship would only grow more harsh, more distant, and more painful.

Amazingly, Winston's devotion to his father never flagged. To him, Lord Randolph always "seemed to own the key to everything or almost everything worth having."[5] Of his father's death in 1895 Winston later wrote, "All my dreams of comradeship with him, of entering Parliament at his side and in his support were ended. There remained for me only to pursue his aims and vindicate his memory."[6] Rather than harbor a cancerous bitterness, Winston chose to allow his father's vision to propel him, chose to give his life to a pleasant continuity rather than a harsh antagonism. Thus, what might have been seeds of self-indulgence and destruction became instead the seeds of greatness, for as Winston himself wrote:

> *Famous men are usually the product of an*
> *unhappy childhood. The stern compression of*
> *circumstances, the twinges of adversity, the spur*
> *of slights and taunts in early years, are needed*
> *to evoke that ruthless fixity of purpose and*
> *tenacious mother wit without which great*
> *actions are seldom accomplished.*[7]

That Winston Churchill modeled "great actions" for generations yet unborn is fairly common knowledge. However, few are aware that he did so strengthened by resolve that sprang from a lonely and potentially crushing childhood, a childhood that might have disheartened and ruined one less willing to cast off bitterness in order to grasp the future.

Self-Education

*"Personally...I am always ready to learn although I
do not always like being taught."* [8]

Teaching is a powerful tool. When it is done well, it can
unleash a people's destiny. But when it is done poorly,
it degenerates into a soul-numbing process that more often
than not kills the spirit of creativity and leadership. Sadly,
many have suffered under this kind of pitiless ineptitude and
one wonders how many brilliant inventors, inspiring writers,
or valiant leaders the world has lost because of it. Winston
Churchill might have been among them.

As a child, Churchill possessed boundless energy and
curiosity. He attacked life with a bold but innocent disregard
for convention, thinking in dimensions few others were able
to perceive, including his teachers. Like all children, he
yearned to understand and please, but his eager mind would
not allow him to march in lock step through a rigid, and at
times senseless, curriculum. Like other men of intelligence
and imagination–Einstein and Edison, for example–he was
labeled "naughty" and "backward" simply because he was
unable to grow in an environment of insipid conformity.

Looking back in later years, Churchill saw what his problem had been: "Where my reason, imagination, or interest were not engaged, I would not or I could not learn."[9] His teachers, as teachers are wont to do, never inspired him with that passion for knowledge so necessary for real learning. The experience marked him.

What he movingly wrote of one institution could have applied to all of his early education: "How I hated this school, and what a life of anxiety I lived there for more than two years. I made very little progress at my lessons, and none at all at games. I counted the days and the hours to the end of every term, when I should return home from this hateful servitude."[10] Not until he entered Sandhurst, where the curriculum was practical and he was no longer hindered by earlier failures, did he achieve distinction as a student. Two triumphant sentences in his autobiography reveal how much success at Sandhurst meant to his educationally battered soul: "Instead of creeping in at the bottom, almost by charity, I passed out with honors eighth in my batch of a hundred and fifty. I mention this because it shows that I could learn quickly enough the things that mattered."[11]

Still, his vibrant curiosity could never be satisfied with the practical lore of military life alone. While stationed in the far-flung British outpost of Bangalore, India, and nearing his twenty-second birthday, he experienced the first stirrings of a driving intellectual curiosity. He came to realize that he regularly used words he could not define and it disturbed him deeply. He found also that there were entire intellectual arenas–like ethics, law, or even the history of England–in which he knew next to nothing "So," he wrote, "I resolved to read history, philosophy, economics, and things like that; and I wrote to my mother asking for such books as I had heard of on these topics."[12] One of the great journeys in self-education had begun.

The journey commenced with Edward Gibbon's eight-volume *Decline and Fall of the Roman Empire* and followed with Gibbon's autobiography. He devoured all of English historian Thomas Babington Macaulay's works, and then plowed through Schopenhauer, Malthus, Darwin, Aristotle, Plato, and Adam Smith. He kept as many as four books going at a time and during the sweltering afternoons of the Indian hot season he read four or five hours a day. He repeatedly read Bartlett's *Familiar Quotations,* memorizing much of it, and he poured over titles like Winwood Reade's *Martyrdom of Man,* Ronald Laing's *Modern Science and Modern Thought,* Henry Hallam's *Constitutional History,* William Lecky's *European Morals* and *Rise and Influence of Rationalism,* Blaise Pascal's *Provincial Letters* and Victor-Henri Rochefort's *Memoirs,* all the while chiding his mother for not keeping him sufficiently supplied.

Even more remarkably, Winston read nearly all of the *Annual Register* and projected himself into the Parliamentary debates it recorded, scribbling his own views into the margins and placing his "vote" before reading the vote of the Members of Parliament. He did this, he wrote his mother, because a "good knowledge of these would arm me with a sharp sword. Macaulay, Gibbon, Plato, etc., must train the muscles to wield that sword to the greatest effect." [13]

"He thus became his own university," wrote Randolph Churchill. [14] But there is more to this than the academic. In honestly facing his weaknesses and devising a plan to overcome them, Churchill came of age, for as William Manchester has written, Churchill's intellectual curiosity "and the means he took to satisfy it, marks the end of his youth and the incipient signs of his emergence as an exceptional man." [15]

The discipline of self-education that Winston so passionately and aggressively practiced during those hot Bangalore afternoons remained with him throughout his life. He read ravenously and broadly, laying the foundation for the kind of leader he would one day be. By doing so, he proved that knowledge does not belong alone to the school or the professional, but to the hungry and the willing, to those who refuse to surrender the power of knowledge or the paths that lead to greatness. It is indeed the mark of "an exceptional man."

COURAGE

"Courage is rightly esteemed the first of human qualities...because it is the quality which guarantees all others." [16]

Courage is a quality that few can define but most recognize when they see it. It is unquestionably a kind of strength that allows men to perform extraordinary feats in the face of overwhelming opposition. It cannot be taught, though it can be inspired, and it normally springs from something like faith or resolve, a commitment to something larger than oneself. It can burst forth instantly, as though awakened by a sudden jolt, but more often it waits in silence until aroused by some pressing challenge. What is certain of courage, though, is that true leadership is impossible without it.

Throughout most of his life, Winston Churchill was a man of exceptional courage. This is hard to account for, though, because his bravery certainly was not a product of physical strength or towering stature. Nor was his childhood the type that produced heroic men. To the contrary, he was neglected, ridiculed, and misused by friends and family alike. In addition, he was brought up in an environment of political machinations and leisure class intrigues that seldom produces principled men of vision. Yet, from as early as his companions could remember, Churchill conducted himself with hardly any regard for personal safety, seemed almost oblivious to criticism where his principles were involved, and repeatedly stood firm before the most concerted opposition.

He once said of himself that he "had a tendency against which I should, perhaps be on my guard, to swim against the stream." [17] This was an understatement. His moral courage was staggering. In his first speech before Parliament he praised his nation's enemies and criticized a senior official of his own party. In one of his first books, he took to task none other than the legendary Lord Herbert Kitchener, most esteemed of all British Army officers, for allowing his troops to desecrate a pagan idol. He was a mere subaltern at the time. He thought nothing of "crossing the aisle" to change political parties, only to change back again when his principles demanded, or chastising his own social class for their heartlessness.

His physical courage was equally astounding. He was almost completely unaware of the chances he took with his own life. In 1897, he risked death to rescue a fellow soldier during fierce fighting on the northwest frontier of India. In the Boer War, while serving only as a journalist, he not only volunteered for a dangerous intelligence mission at the Battle of Diamond Hill, but was later captured while trying to rescue men who were trapped during a Boer attack. Early in the First World War, when the Germans were about to occupy Antwerp and the Belgians were planning to evacuate, Churchill risked his life by going to the city in support of its defenders. Later, when he was dismissed from the Admiralty after the Dardanelles disaster, Churchill resigned from the cabinet, took a commission as a colonel, and assumed command of a battalion fighting in the trenches on the western front. He was over 40 years old at the time.

While he was staying with friends at an ancient country home near Ockham, a heating system exploded into flames during the night. The screaming guests were led to the lawn for safety. All except one. Churchill's friend Eddie Marsh later wrote, "Winston commandeered a fireman's helmet and assumed the direction of operations." [18] Churchill mounted the roof of the blazing structure and led firemen in a valiant but futile attempt to extinguish the blaze with a tiny fire engine brought from the nearby town. Despite their efforts, the house was lost. Guests eventually forgot the tragedy, but never the vision of the little man who stood on the roof of a burning house dressed only in a bathrobe and fire helmet.

During the war years, he repeatedly inspired the British people with his nerve. His favorite place to wait out Nazi air raids was on the rooftops of government buildings. During one Christmas, he flew to Athens where he brought together the warring parties of the Greek civil war, all the while under pressing hostile fire. Once when his car was passing through Hyde Park, several suspicious men began to approach. Inspector Thompson, Churchill's bodyguard, noticed the men immediately and the car was stopped. The momentary silence was broken when Churchill, fingering the Colt automatic he always kept with him, calmly but firmly declared, "If they want trouble they can have it." Before the Prime Minister could act, though, Thompson told the driver: "Step on it; drive like the Devil." [19] The crisis was averted, but Churchill was, as usual, both ready and fearless. On November 14, 1940, as Churchill was driving out of London, a motorcyclist stopped the car to say that the Luftwaffe was headed for London. It would have made perfect sense for the Prime Minister of England to remain outside the city until the attack was over.

Instead, Churchill ordered the car back to London, back into the falling bombs.

Churchill holds an honored place in history largely because he inspired steely courage during a catastrophic global conflict. To assume, though, that he was merely giving voice to the British lion, that somehow he demanded virtues of his people that he did not possess himself, is to miss the most important dynamic of his brand of leadership. Churchill only asked of others what he required of himself. He asked people to risk their lives, as he had done, to protect their civilization. He asked them to suffer for their principles as he had done time and again. He asked them to stare terror in the face without flinching, something he knew all too well how to do. For Churchill, leadership was not theater, not the assumption of a role far different from who he really was. His was leadership by example, by an authority gained through superior commitment and sacrifice, and by courage thoroughly tested in the fires of experience.

ACTION

"Things do not get better by being left alone. Unless they are adjusted, they explode with a shattering detonation." [20]

In his poem, *Psalm Of Life*, Henry Wadsworth Longfellow wrote of man's need for action.

> *Not enjoyment, and not sorrow,*
> *Is our destined end or way;*
> *But to act, that each to-morrow*
> *Find us farther than to-day*
> *Trust no Future, howe'er pleasant!*
> *Let the dead Past bury its dead!*
> *Act,–act in the living Present!*
> *Heart within, and God o'erhead!*

This poem was one of Churchill's favorites and it wonderfully captures his view of life. In fact, the word that best describes Churchill is *action*. Even from his youth, he was addicted to movement. William Manchester records that when

Winston was "not lost in thought, he was in constant motion, jumping up and down, leaping from chair to chair, rushing about, and falling and hurting himself."[21] In school, his hyperactive nature and yearning for adventure brought him into unceasing conflict with authorities. The routine and the tedious repelled him. Where other subjects failed to spark his interest, though, the drama and motion of history seized him and held him transfixed. Then, as he grew older, the bold pageantry and sweeping action of the military stirred him, as did the thrust and parry of politics. He could never keep himself from the energy of passion and power.

Yet, Churchill's zeal for doing grew out of more than mere physical drive. Action was his philosophy of life. He believed instinctively that men's affairs tend toward decline apart from bold and decisive action. For him, passivity and neglect were sins. Things are only improved by action, by taking matters in hand and "doing something." "I never worry about action," he said, "but only about inaction."[22]

Churchill's experience in life taught him that victory is won by concentrated and undying effort. He overcame the frail physique that brought him so much bullying in school by mastering fencing and swimming. They demanded hour after hour of devoted practice. He then overcame his huge gaps in his learning by becoming his own teacher. He planned the curriculum, acquired the materials, and worked himself night and day until he was satisfied. He also built his career by positioning himself in the dangerous hot spots of the world and carving out a reputation for bravery. To execute all of this required that he have a goal, a plan, and an iron will. Finally, in his greatest test, the one against the Nazis, he knew before most other leaders did that doing nothing would be disastrous. Bold, creative, commanding, unswerving action was the tall order of the day and Churchill was prepared to answer it.

As a man of action, though, nothing frustrated him quite like uncertain, passive leaders. During the 1930's, when he was out of power but forced to witness the ill-conceived policies of appeasement, he said of its architects that they were. "Decided only to be undecided, resolved to be irresolute, adamant for drift, solid for fluidity, all powerful to be impotent." [23] "Why wouldn't they act?" he wondered, until upon reflection he began to understand.

First, they lacked the will. Churchill knew that victory graces those whose basic attitude is action and strength rather than vacillation and meekness, that even knowing what to do is not enough without the will to do it. "It is one thing to see the forward path," he believed, "and another to be able to take it." [24] It is a simple philosophy, perhaps, but the simplicity makes taking the first step easier: "If you travel the earth, you will find it is largely divided into two classes of people–people who say 'I wonder why such and such is not done' and people who say 'Now who is going to prevent me from doing that thing?'" [25]

Second, they lacked a plan. Even if one possessed the will to act, it would not be enough without a plan. "It is better to have an ambitious plan than none at all," he believed, and he spent large amounts of time planning in anticipation of crises while those without wise planning were overwhelmed and immobilized by events. [26]

Third, they wanted perfection. Without it, they would do nothing. Churchill knew that any policy or battle plan has to be fine-tuned once in progress, so he never expected perfection from the beginning. He mobilized while others micro-managed because he understood that the details could be changed later; the critical need was action. "The maxim, 'Nothing avails but perfection,'" he said, "may be spelled, Paralysis." [27]

Armed with these insights into the mistakes of others, Churchill was ready when the call for wise, decisive action sounded. It was then he might have quoted, as he often did at great length, from his dear Longfellow:

> *Let us, then, be up and doing,*
> *With a heart for any fate;*
> *Still achieving, still pursuing,*
> *Learn to labor and to wait.*

The Bible

"We may be sure that all these things happened just as they are set according to Holy Writ. We may believe that they happened to people not so very different from ourselves, and that the impressions those people received were faithfully recorded and have been transmitted across the centuries with far more accuracy than many of the telegraphed accounts we read of the goings-on of today. In the words of a forgotten work of Mr. Gladstone, we rest with assurance upon 'The Impregnable Rock of Holy Scripture.'" [28]

It is difficult for people living at the end of the twentieth century to understand how the King James Bible revolutionized the English-speaking world. For more than three hundred years, the Authorized Version virtually *was* Protestant Christianity. Through it the images of Christian spirituality, the beauty of the English language, and the power of the Gospel of Christ were disseminated throughout the world. No man was thought educated who had not mastered it; no nation civilized without its influence. For generations its language defined the greatness of Christianity and its fire aroused the greatness in the advancing armies of Christian civilization.

Few great leaders in recent memory have clung to the Bible as tenaciously as Winston Churchill. Though historians have largely ignored the influence of the King James Bible on Churchill's style and thinking, there is little question that from the days of Mrs. Everest on, it was of immense importance. Even during his school years, in which he won numerous awards for memorizing Scripture, the drama and Elizabethan phrasing of the Bible captivated him. This continued throughout his life and he often astounded his audiences by the lengthy passages of Scripture he could quote from memory and by how moved he could be by the slightest reference to the word of God.

The language of Scripture even shaped his own writing style: an army, for example, was not large, but "in number as the sands of the sea." [29] And his speeches were punctuated with Scriptural references. In his first speech to the House of Commons, after becoming Prime Minister at the outbreak of World War II, he movingly cited First Maccabees of the Apocrypha: "Arm yourselves, and be ye men of valour, and be in readiness for the conflict; for it is better for us to perish in battle than to look upon the outrage of our nation. As the will of God is in Heaven, even so let it be." [30]

Though he praised the King James Bible as a "lasting monument . . . to the genius of the English-speaking peoples," he also understood its supernatural power. [31] In critical moments throughout their lives both Winston and Clementine found comfort and guidance in its pages. On one occasion, during 1911, when he was hoping to be appointed First Lord of the Admiralty, Winston confessed to Clementine that he feared he might not be chosen. She was confident he would:

"I know it's all right about the Admiralty," she replied.[32] Her confidence came from prayerfully opening her grandmother's Bible and landing upon Psalm 107:23-24.[33]

> *They that go down to the sea in ships*
> *that do business in great waters;*
> *these see the works of the Lord,*
> *and his wonders in the deep.*

She was right, for Winston was indeed chosen. But the task that faced him was almost overwhelming, and when he needed some sense of divine confirmation and direction, he also turned to his Bible. He landed upon the ninth chapter of Deuteronomy, which is of particular interest since Churchill was just about to lead the entire British Navy into a world war.

> *Hear, O Israel: Thou art to pass over Jordan this*
> *day, to go in to possess nations greater and*
> *mightier than thyself...Understand therefore*
> *this day, that the Lord thy God is he which*
> *goeth over before thee; as a consuming fire he*
> *shall destroy them, and he shall bring them*
> *down before thy face; so shall thou drive them*
> *out, and destroy them quickly, as the Lord hath*
> *said unto thee.*

These episodes are not unusual in Churchill's life. He read the Bible repeatedly throughout his lifetime and often discussed its meaning with his staff and friends. He had, his intimates knew, an "inner relationship" with the Bible, and so they were not surprised by his emotional response when the Chief Rabbi of Palestine presented him with a Scroll of the Law atop Mount

Scopus in Jerusalem. Before the thousands of Jews who had assembled, Churchill was undone. With tears streaming down his face and the Torah clutched tightly in his hands, he promised, "This sacred book which contains truth accepted by Jews and Christians alike is very dear to me, and your gift will remain in my family as an imperishable souvenir." [34]

Politicians routinely use Scripture to cynically play upon their nation's Christian memory. Churchill's use of Scripture was different. He genuinely believed in the inspiration and truth of the Bible, and he knew its power to order his private world. That he could be such a momentous leader was due in part to the fact that he in turn was led by a truth beyond himself: the truth of holy Scripture.

Destiny

"There has to be a purpose to it all. I believe that I was chosen for a purpose far beyond our simple reasoning." [35]

In earlier, more Christian eras, men believed they were moved by a force that today, in our world of evolution and random chance, is taken for arrogance and license. It was the power of predestination, of God's choosing and ordaining every life for a purpose. Found first in Scripture, it was expanded by Augustine, revived by the Reformers, and has since inspired generations to bold faith and action. Untold numbers have been moved to attempt what on their own strength, without the guarantee of a fixed destiny, they would never have begun.

Winston Churchill lived the first twenty-seven years of his life in the Victorian era, an age still rooted in the Christian understanding of the world. The idea of destiny, of a purpose ordained before the beginning of history, figured decisively in men's thoughts and actions. It is not surprising, then, that Churchill, who drank as deeply as any man from the Victorian well, perceived his life in the light of an overriding providence, in terms of a divinely appointed purpose.

In *My Early Life*, Churchill wrote of his "conclusion upon Free Will and Predestination." He determined, he said, "that they are identical." [36] It is a telling statement. The man who believes this must have already heard the drumbeat of his destiny. He must have felt it flowing through him and put it to the test. He believes that the choices he makes merely accomplish the purposes set for his life. It makes him bold and courageous. He has confidence he will achieve his destiny and that death will not come until it is fulfilled.

This was Churchill, who even in battle, when most men contemplate the frailty of life, was not shaken from his sense of destiny. During the South African War, he wrote, "These are anxious days, but when one is quite sure that one is filling one's proper place in the scheme of the world affairs, one may await events with entire composure." [37] Still later, during World War I, he wrote to Clementine, "I am superior to anything that can happen to me out here. My conviction that the greatest of my work is still to be done is strong within me." [38] "Over me beat unseen wings," [39] he assured her. "I believe I am to be pre-served for future things." [40]

Churchill's life does suggest the influence of a guiding hand. He wrote in *Thoughts and Adventures*, "If we look back on our past life we shall see that one of its most usual experiences is that we have been helped by our mistakes and injured by our most sagacious decisions." [41] This was the story of his life. As a Harrow student taking the entrance exam for Sandhurst, he knew that geography would be a major part of the test. He decided to cut the nations of the world out of a map, put them in a hat, and choose one at random to focus on in his preparations. He chose New Zealand. On exam day, the first assignment was "Draw a Map of New Zealand," which he did, right down to the "parks, the libraries, and even the tram lines." [42] He earned the full points and squeaked into Sandhurst. During his escape from a Boer prison camp in South Africa, he had the good fortune to give himself up to the one British home within miles. At any other he would have been captured and returned–"dead or alive." During World War I, a visiting general called him out of his billet for an unscheduled inspection. As soon as he left, shellfire destroyed the billet and everything in the vicinity. [43] His life was so filled with such near misses and near disasters turned blessings that it is difficult to avoid his conclusion: "This cannot be accident, it must be design." [44]

Moreover, Churchill's sense of destiny was at times almost mystical. He seemed to know when the forces of destiny were about to touch him, how a divine symmetry might shape his life. As he left for the South African War, he wrote, "I have a feeling, a sort of intuition, that if I go something will come of it." [45] His intuition was correct. The fame he acquired by escaping from the Boer prison camp allowed him to make a successful run for Parliament, though before the war he had been soundly defeated in the same endeavor. Even more startling was when he told a friend, decades before his death, "Today is the twenty-fourth of January. It is the day my father died. It is the day that I shall die too." [46] And, indeed, on January 24, 1965, his destiny fulfilled, he left this life.

Thus, when he became Prime Minister at the onset of World War II, it was no surprise that his thoughts turned to the path his life had taken up to that moment. "I felt as if I were walking with destiny," he wrote in his *Second World War*, "and that all my past life had been but a preparation for this hour and for this trial." [47] He knew the power of destiny. He knew "that a man's own contribution to his life story is continually dominated by an external superior power." And because he knew it he served his nation with a brand of leadership far grander than would be possible for one who saw himself merely as a product of political processes. For Churchill, leadership was much more than politics; it was the impact of everything he was destined to be upon the times in which he was destined to live.

MARRIAGE

"At times, I think I could conquer everything–and then again I know I am only a weak vain fool. But your love for me is the greatest glory and recognition that has or will ever befall me: and the attachment which I feel towards you is not capable of being altered by the sort of things that happen in this world. I only wish I were more worthy of you and more able to meet the inner needs of your soul." [48]

We no longer live when public men are measured by the quality of their marriages. "Men of affairs" today are often just that and the greater the distance they can place between themselves and their crumbling home lives the better. For some unclear reason, the inability of a man to loyally fulfill his vows to his wife is no longer taken as indication of the character with which he will serve the public. Our age has suffered for embracing such folly. In Winston Churchill's age, though, a public man's marriage was more than a well-rehearsed drama, it was the yardstick by which the moral measure of the man was taken. Thus, it was often said of

Churchill what is announced of today's leaders only with a wink of cynicism: "Winston Churchill loved his wife." Little else is as revealing of his character.

When 34-year-old Churchill married Clementine Hozier, he was already a war hero, author, and statesman. With a renowned ancestry and an international reputation, he was a man on the rise in Parliament. Clementine, ten years his junior, was the product of a shattered marriage and an unstable home life. Yet, she had been educated at the Sorbornne, possessed "classical" beauty, and was known to be an excellent tennis player and a good hunter, "for a woman."

They appeared to be as opposite as a husband and wife could be. She was an early riser who retired early in the evening. He worked until 3 a.m. and then slept late. She was an inveterate worrier. He took risks whenever possible and loved daring adventure. She was of Scots descent and believed in frugal ways and plain living. Money problems made her nervous. Winston, on the other hand, spent money like there was no end to it and kept the family in perpetual arrears. He enjoyed raucous parties and loud dinner guests with strong opinions. She found them crude and unsettling and sometimes even ordered guests out of her house (Winston said she once descended on a man "like a jaguar from a tree"). He had boundless energy; she was often tired and in constant need of rest. He loved Chartwell, their home in Kent; the work on the house, the development of the land, the entertaining. She found it ostentatious and too much work. He expressed everything, wept freely, and lavished affection upon her. She kept everything bottled up until the pressure became too much and she exploded, much to the astonishment of her family and friends.

This strange mixture seems a sure prescription for divorce, but somehow Winston and Clementine melded their differences into one of the most movingly intimate marriages on record. Together they created a realm of supportive intimacy that filled the void in each of their lives. It was a private realm, adorned with gentleness and a level of acceptance neither had known before. As one historian has written, "There would always be a place in their relationship into which no one else would enter."[49] From the time of their honeymoon, during which they "loitered and loved," they together built a safe haven that would forever be their private refuge.

Within this world only pet names were used. He was "Mr. Pug" or "Pig" and she, "Mrs. Kat." The children were called "kittens" and were given names like "Chumbolly" and "Duckadilly." Unborn children were "Puppy Kittens." When one of them entered the house, some absurd sound–like a nasal "Wonk! Wonk!"–would be made, with the entire family, from whatever quarter, repeating the sound in greeting. Their displays of affection were public and unrestrained. There was abundant wrestling, slapping, holding, and tickling in their home. On Churchill's birthday, a visiting Lord found "Kat" and "Pig," attired in paper hats, purring cat-like at each other on a sofa. They delighted in caring for each other. If a wasp landed on Clementine, Winston, knowing her deathly fear, would gallantly grab the insect and cast it into a nearby fire. Then he would turn to her and ask with deepest concern, "Did you survive, my Kat?" as though they had together confronted the dragon of St. George.

Their letters reveal an almost adolescent sentimentality. He might address her as "my beautiful white pussy cat." If he had just left on a plane he might write that he had "a touching vision of you and your kittens growing rapidly smaller." He was "eternally attached to her" and pledged, "I want to be worthy of all the beauties of your nature. It gives me so much joy to make you happy."[50] Clementine was equally expressive in writing, far more so than in person. When she had once been rude to one of their house guests, she wrote in apology, "My sweet and Dear Pig, when I am a withered old woman how miserable I shall be if I have disturbed your life and troubled your spirit by my temper. Do not cease to love me. I could not do without it." [51] Often, their letters included drawings of pigs, kittens, hearts, and other symbols of endearment. These exchanges might easily be mistaken for the lovesick scrawlings of teenagers were they not signed by the Prime Minister of Great Britain.

What is most astounding about the marriage of Winston and Clementine is that–far from immune to the pressures that shipwreck the marriages of others–they experienced almost every disadvantage in outsized proportion. By modern standards they were doomed from the beginning. There was no degree of loneliness, anger, rejection, pain, bitterness, or opportunity for unfaithfulness that they did not experience. But in their more than 55 years together, they endured largely because they admitted their inadequacies, fed their intimacy at any cost, and understood their marriage in the sustaining light of eternity. So, as Winston wrote in the very last line of his autobiographical *My Early Life*, "I married...and lived happily ever afterwards." [52]

CRITICISM

"In one respect a cavalry charge is very like ordinary life. So long as you are all right, firmly in your saddle, your horse in hand, and well armed, lots of enemies will give you wide berth. But as soon as you have lost a stirrup, have a rein cut, have dropped your weapon, are wounded, or your horse is wounded, then is the moment when from all quarters enemies rush upon you." [53]

One of the deciding marks of a great leader is the way he handles criticism. Leadership is, after all, a matter of things like standing for principle, exercising authority, and marshaling resources, change, and power–the very things most likely to invite criticism. The mettle of a leader is tested by the criticism he receives. He cannot afford to ignore it or become preoccupied with it. Nor can he allow a root of bitterness to set in that threatens to warp his judgment. Instead, he has to look fully at the criticism lodged against him, however harsh or unjust it may be, draw from it what wisdom he can, and move on.

Winston Churchill was the kind of man people loved to criticize. His ego and jaunty self-confidence, his rather strange appearance, his lisp, his explosive personality, and his unusual habits offered his critics a target too tempting to ignore. What really drew the barbs, though, was that Churchill was a man of resolute principle, for nothing draws opposition quite like the settled confidence that grows from knowing one is right.

Churchill assumed from the start that strong leaders automatically draw criticism: "People who are not prepared to do unpopular things and to defy clamor," he said, "are not fit to be Ministers in times of stress."[54] He could handle his critics, though, as long as he was at peace with himself, as long as he knew he was doing the right thing: "The only guide to a man is his conscience," he said upon the death of Neville Chamberlain, "the only shield to his memory is the rectitude and the sincerity of his actions. It is very imprudent to walk through life without this shield, because we are so often mocked by the failure of our hopes and the upsetting of our calculations; but with this shield, however the fates may play, we march always in the ranks of honor." Churchill walked with uncommon confidence because he walked as a man of conscience. Others may have taken it as arrogance when he said things like, "I have no intention of passing my remaining years in explaining or withdrawing anything I have said in the past, still less in apologizing for it," but this is actually the boldness of a principled man.[55]

That is not to say that Churchill refused to learn from the rebukes he incurred. "Criticism in the body politic," he said, "is like pain in the human body. It is not pleasant, but where would the body be without it?"[56] Though not quite like E. Stanley Jones in his attitude toward critics—"My critics are the unpaid guardians of my soul," Jones said—Churchill was very much like Marcus Aurelius, who wrote in his *Meditations*, "When another blames or hates you, or when men say injurious things about you, approach their poor souls, penetrate within, and see what kind of men they are. You will discover that there is no reason to take trouble that these men have a good opinion of you. However, you must be well disposed towards them, for by nature they are friends." [57]

As a man of action, what really disturbed Churchill was criticism by people who sat on the sidelines. "Criticism is easy," he said, "achievement is difficult." [58] Particularly during the war years he endured incessant attacks from groups that refused to lift a finger in the cause. It inflamed him: "It is not open to the cool bystander...to set himself up as an impartial judge of events which would never have occurred had he outstretched a helping hand in time." [59] Churchill believed that the voice of criticism had to earn its way, that there were dues to be paid before winning the right to be heard. He had paid them. He expected others to, as well.

He was particularly disturbed when politicians went to ludicrous extremes to avoid the slings and arrows of taking a stand. He believed that the policies of appeasement, which he opposed so eloquently in the 1930's, resulted not only from moral weakness and shortsightedness, but also from fear of offending a misguided public. Churchill believed leaders had to act according to their best instincts: "Nothing is more dangerous in wartime than to live in the temperamental atmosphere of a Gallup Poll, always feeling one's pulse and taking one's temperature." [60] But Churchill also was concerned about leaders who allowed public opinion to move them to action prematurely. He had seen "war fever" drive nations to destruction in the "Great War," and he believed leaders ought to know better: "Let us learn our lessons. Never, never, never believe any war will be smooth and easy, or that anyone who embarks on the strange voyage can measure the tides and hurricanes he will encounter. The Statesman who yields to war fever must realize that once the signal is given, he is no longer the master of policy but the slave of unforeseeable and uncontrollable events."[61]

Churchill was not immune to the pain of criticism. He spoke from experience when he said "Politics is almost as exciting as war and quite as dangerous. In war you can only be killed once; in politics many times."[62] But he knew that true leadership automatically generates criticism, that opposition is the natural environment of effective leaders, and that resisting extreme reaction to criticism is the key to steadiness at the helm. In fact, it seemed at times that Churchill used criticism as a kind of guidance system, that he took it as confirmation of a right course. Scripture says that a man is tested by the praise he receives. Churchill knew that criticism can be of equal value.

CHANGE

"To improve is to change; to be perfect is to change often." [63]

By nature, human beings shrink from change. Change seems to stir our insecurities as it forces us from the familiar into unsettling confrontation with the new. Wrongly, we equate change with loss. Psychologists say that because we subconsciously want to return to the stability and warmth of the womb, we gravitate to the comfortable and the routine. But life is change, and true success in any field is largely a matter of learning how to anticipate change, how to harness it, and how to ride its power into the future.

When Winston Churchill was born on November 30, 1874, electricity, radio, television, and telephones were unknown. Benjamin Disraeli had just become Prime Minister of England and Queen Victoria still reigned, as she would for another twenty-seven years. There were men living who had fought Napoleon. In America, Ulysses S. Grant was in his second term as President. Karl Marx was in the British Library writing the *Communist Manifesto* and Mark Twain had not written most of the works for which he would become famous. Tennis was in its infancy and Yale, Princeton, Columbia, and Rutgers Universities had met only the year before to draw up the first rules for a game called football.

When Churchill died ninety years later, on January 24, 1965, the world was quite a different place. That year, men orbited the earth, walked in space, and sent a space probe to the surface of Venus. Pictures from Mars were beamed 134 million miles back to earth by *Mariner IV*. An automobile was driven over 600 miles per hour, satellite links were in operation between the United States and Europe, and sex-change operations were a reality. Nuclear power had come of age. The American president at the time was Lyndon Johnson, who, though considered an elderly man, was born when Churchill was already thirty-four. Johnson was but one of the nineteen presidents who served during Winston's lifetime, a span which also included six British monarchs and twenty-eight prime ministers. That same year, the Beatles went to Buckingham Palace to receive the Order of the British Empire from Queen Elizabeth II. Churchill also received this honor, but for an entirely different contribution in an entirely different age.

Change was an ever-present challenge in Churchill's life and it frequently filled his thoughts.

> *I wonder often whether any other generation has seen such astounding revolutions of data and values as those through which we have lived. Scarcely anything material or established which I was brought up to believe was permanent and vital, has lasted. Everything I was sure or taught to be sure was impossible, has happened.*[64]

Had Churchill regarded all change with dread and fore-boding, he might have passed his days in a nostalgic paralysis. For him, though, change was no enemy: it was opportunity-and he intended to seize it. He valued tradition and heritage as much as any man of his age, but he refused to be enticed into a wistful nostalgia. History was about progress–and whatever the future held, it would be led by those who conquered their innate fear of the unknown and determined that for them change meant advance.

Nothing demonstrates Churchill's ability to embrace "the new" more dramatically than his mastery of military tech-nology. Churchill rode in Victorian-era cavalry charges when the lance was a weapon of choice. Yet, when he inherited an antiquated British Navy as First Lord of the Admiralty prior to World War I, he wasted no time in preparing for the future. He dismissed mossbacked admirals and replaced outdated ships. He ordered the Navy to switch its fuel from coal to oil, a crit-ical decision which gave British ships the winning edge in speed and efficiency. He also introduced the fifteen-inch high-explosive gun, without which the Navy would have been fatally out-gunned and out-maneuvered. True to form, when war broke out, he had already foreseen it and the fleet had been long at sea by the time Churchill received official notice of hostilities.

Churchill not only used change: he created it. Prior to World War I, he instructed naval engineers to explore the idea of an armored car designed to scale trenches. He thus became the father of the modern tank, or "Winston's folly," as critics then called it. In 1912, moved by his belief that aviation was "most important," he formed the Royal Naval Air Service, which later became the Royal Flying Corps and then the Royal Air Force. Britain became the first country to equip a plane with a machine gun and launch an airborne torpedo because of his efforts. During World War II, Churchill first suggested the idea of the artificial harbors used at Normandy. He proposed that bombers drop strips of tinfoil to confuse enemy radar, pioneered the idea of building a pipeline under the ocean, and invented a device called a "Gee" for guiding pilots.

"The only way a man can remain consistent amid changing circumstance," he wrote in the middle of his life, "is to change with them while preserving the same dominating purpose."[65] Change tactics and methods, he believed, but never principles. So, whether he was switching political parties, devising strategies to accommodate the shifting tides of war, or harnessing the latest in technology, Churchill made change serve his vision. He learned to love it and to welcome the demands it made. This attitude distinguished him among men of his or any other generation, and it is part of the command of historical forces that so marked his leadership.

DUTY

"The destiny of mankind is not decided by material computation. When great causes are on the move in the world...we learn that we are spirits, not animals, and that something is going on in space and time, and beyond space and time, which, whether we like it or not, spells duty." [66]

The word duty sounds almost foreign to modern ears. The very idea assumes more than our age has to offer. It assumes that there is an order to life, that individuals have a role to play in that order, and that there are matters of greater importance than personal pleasure and fulfillment. It assumes also that men have an obligation to each other and that the good of the many rightly demands sacrifice from the few. More importantly, it assumes that there are noble causes to which men must be pledged in order to be noble themselves.

Earlier generations were familiar with the idea of duty. When Admiral Nelson signaled the fleet at the Battle of Trafalgar that "England expects every man will do his duty," every seaman knew what was required of him. Nelson's words and the heroic tale of this battle entered the lore of Great Britain to be passed down from generation to generation as a call to duty. In the United States, duty was not just a word blustery speechmakers used on patriotic occasions. It was an idea fathers embedded in the hearts of their sons, a standard that measured manhood, character, and leadership.

The call of duty rang loudest in hearts of faith. People who believed that life draws its meaning from eternity and that men live not for rewards in this world but in the next–people such as this understood duty as that body of works God had prepared for them "from before the foundations of the world." Phrases like "sacred duty," "God-given duty," and "the duty of all men" fell freely from the lips of men in every station of life. Somehow the idea of duty transformed, making mundane tasks noble and common lives extraordinary.

Of all the pudgy, rosy-cheeked British children who heard of Nelson and his stirring charge in the nurseries and play-rooms of England, none was as affected as young Winston Churchill. He was, after all, a descendant of the Duke of Marlborough and the son of a member of Queen Victoria's Parliament. His early training, largely at the knee of his beloved nanny, taught him that privilege of birth demanded exceptional devotion and sacrifice. They called it *noblesse oblige*, the idea that nobility obligates, that to whom much is given, much is required in return. Churchill learned it well and it was a guide to him during his rich life of public service.

One of the mysteries of Churchill's life is that time and again, when he might have easily pursued less bruising occupations or settled into a life of ease, he kept reaching for the power to shape events. Historians normally interpret this as ego and a "will to power" manifested only by the slightly deranged. This is the easy answer, though, informed more by cynicism than truth. The fact is that Churchill, like most men of his generation, his class, and his faith, saw himself as born with a responsibility to do good. Suspect in our age, perhaps, but a matter of gospel in Churchill's.

At the turn of the century, Churchill turned from what might have been a promising career and ran for Parliament. In the 1930's, when the British people and their leaders blindly refused to rise to the Nazi threat, Churchill never stopped working to avert the inevitable. Even when the war was won and British voters resoundingly threw him out of office, the former prime minister could not shake his sense of duty: "If I stay on for the time being, bearing the burden at my age, it is not because of love of power or office. I have had an ample feast of both. If I stay it is because I have the feeling that I may, through things that have happened, have an influence on what I care about above all else–the building of a sure and lasting peace." [67]

Yet nothing exceeds the sense of duty Churchill exhibited in hanging on to his second term as prime minister. Well into his late seventies, a recent victim of a very serious stroke and with his family pleading daily for him to resign, Churchill stubbornly refused to leave. Pundits thought he was past it, Anthony Eden thought he stayed on only to deny him his shot at prime minister, and others decided that his power hungry hands would have to be pried off of the controls of state. Churchill didn't care what they thought. He knew his duty: "If I remain in public life at this juncture, it is because, rightly or wrongly, but sincerely, I believe that I may be able to make an important contribution to the prevention of a third world war and to bring nearer that lasting peace settlement which the masses of people of every race and in every land so fervently desire." [68]

Moved by an overriding sense of duty himself, Churchill knew how to help other men hear its call as well. *Duty* is one of the most-often used words in his speeches because he believed that if good men of pure intent unswervingly did their duty, victory would follow. To do so was to play the part Providence had ordained, to walk in the pathway of destiny. Therefore, men ought to "dread naught when duty calls." When the telling moment arrived, all that was required was to "stand erect and look the world in the face and do our duty without fear or favor." [69]

Churchill's sense of duty lifted him above the comfort and self-absorption that satisfied other men. Undoubtedly, he loved his pleasures and all that the fruits of his labors provided. But the measure of the man is that he was willing to lay aside the very things he loved for a higher cause. "We make a living by what we get," he believed, "We make a life by what we give." [70] This is the attitude that distinguished Churchill and other men like him: he wanted a life, not just an existence. He wanted to make his mark, do his bit, play his role, and know that he had "walked in the paths of greatness." To merely exist was no better than death. But to live the vital existence of one who rises to duty, who takes in hand the gauntlet of destiny, this is a life worth the trouble and worthy of emulation.

FAMILY

"There is no doubt that it is around the family and the home that all the greatest virtues, the most dominating virtues of human society, are created, strengthened and maintained." [71]

It was Christmas Eve in 1941 and Winston Churchill was in Washington D.C. as a guest of President Roosevelt. After a busy schedule that included addressing a joint session of Congress and lighting the White House Christmas tree, Churchill retired early in the evening to prepare for a much needed night of sleep.

Also in the White House on this Christmas Eve was Diana Hopkins, the nine-year-old daughter of presidential aide Harry Hopkins. Late in the evening, Diana heard a knock on her door. "Miss Hopkins," the White House butler said gravely, "the Prime Minister wants to see you." The little girl sleepily pulled on her robe and followed the stately butler to the Monroe Bedroom. The butler knocked on the door, prompting a gruff, indistinguishable response from within. When the door opened, Diana looked up to see the kind but penetrating eyes of Winston Churchill staring down at her. Suddenly, Churchill reached out his arms and warmly embraced the stunned child. "I'm a lonely old father and grandfather on Christmas Eve who wanted a little girl to hug," he explained, and then sheepishly sent her back to bed.

This is a side of Winston Churchill few people know. Images of Churchill the war leader, the award-winning author, the master speechmaker, or the astute politician come easily; but not images of Churchill the devoted father or grandfather–not the kind of man who might need a little girl's hug on a lonely Christmas Eve. This is tragic, for he was indeed a tender and devoted father and it is important that this part of his life be remembered as well.

His own childhood was horribly lacking in affection. Young Winston was usually treated as an inconvenience, his parents too busy climbing the social ladder to give him the attention he deserved. He, in turn, worshipped them. Of his mother he wrote, "she shone for me like the evening star–I loved her dearly, but at a distance."[72] It was worse with his father, about whom he learned more from the press than from relationship. It is not hard to imagine how he determined in his heart that with his own children it would be different.

And it was. Churchill adored his children and in the early years the family home was filled with love and good-natured rowdiness. The start of a typical day at home found Winston grabbing one of the children and wrestling them for what he considered his share of kisses. He loved the times of rough play with the children even more than they did and infused them with the same passion he had for the rest of life. One of the family's favorite games was "gorilla." Wearing his old clothes, Winston hid in a tree or in bushes until one of the children appeared. He then lunged out at the unsuspecting child with a loud growl. His nephew recalled that "we squealed with delight and enjoyed this exclusive performance hugely. Few people can say that they have seen an ex-First Lord of the Admiralty crouching in the branches of an oak, baring his teeth and pounding his chests with his fists." Randolph remembered that when his father emerged from hiding "we would all scatter in various directions. He would pursue us and the one he caught would be the loser."[73]

On another occasion, the children and their cousins built a bridge with a Meccano set, a kind of Erector set. Winston appeared on the scene and took stock of the situation. "Hmmm. A bascule bridge would be better, you know," he said thoughtfully. One of the children explained that there were not enough pieces for such a feat. Winston immediately summoned a servant and sent her to buy several Meccano boxes. The children recalled later that he "took off his coat and began preparing the largest model bascule bridge ever...The final construction was a gigantic piece of engineering some fifteen feet long and eight feet high, with a roadway which could be lifted by means of wheels, pulleys, and yards of string."[74] Truly, a Churchillian approach to play!

Amidst the storms and hurried pace of his life, Churchill tried to give himself to his children. He remembered to bring home gifts for them and took them on trips when he could. He even wrote songs and poems for them. Amusingly, they were never spanked because the great war hero couldn't bring himself to do it. Instead, when they angered him he simply banished the children from his presence. These times of punishment were few, though, since normally he doted on his children. During a holiday when Randolph was home from Eton, he told his son, "I have talked to you more in this holiday than my father talked to me in his whole life." It was true, and it was painful, but thankfully Winston's children gave him the kind of joy he had never known in his own childhood.

The lesson here is not that Churchill was the best of fathers; actually, he was gone from home far more than was best for the family. Nor is the point that Churchill's children were perfect; each suffered from the flaws and excesses one might expect. Yet, the important truth is that Churchill tried; that, in spite of all his staggering pressures and global responsibilities, he loved his children, worked to give them a good life, and hoped to successfully launch them toward destinies of their own. However his children may have turned out, they never lacked for a caring father–and for this Churchill should be remembered, as much if not more than for any other qualities he possessed.

HISTORY

*" The greatest advances in human civilization have
come when we recovered what we had lost: when we
learned the lessons of history."* [75]

Thomas Fuller, the English divine and historian, once
wrote, "History maketh a man old, without either wrin-
kles or gray hairs; privileging him with the experience of age,
without either the infirmities or inconveniences thereof." [76]
Strong leaders throughout the centuries have learned to gain
the "experience of age," and even of the ages, by learning
what the past has to teach. History has the power to lift a
leader out of the shortsightedness of his own times and give
him the perspective of centuries. From this view, the problems
of any one age seem less daunting and the real issues of man's
existence gain focus. Instructed by his experience with the
past, a leader can then throw open the windows of his age to
what C. S. Lewis called "the clean sea-breeze of the centuries."

When people speak of Winston Churchill as a historian,
they usually refer to his many books, or his Pulitzer Prize, or
his experiences on the front lines of history. But Churchill was

a historian in a deeper, more meaningful, sense. History was the way he understood the world, the lens he used to bring reality into focus. Churchill thought historically, meaning that he understood life in terms of generations, great men, the succession of ages, heroic events, noble conflicts, and the linear connections of time. For him history was more than something to study; it was a way of thinking. As Lord Ismay, Churchill's chief of staff, said, Churchill "thought in terms of history all the time. He felt that the light of history played upon all that we did, and he acted accordingly." [77]

Churchill was fascinated with the light of history from an early age. It was the one subject that stirred his active imagination in school. He refused to be bothered with his other studies but in history he astounded his teachers by reading well beyond his years and by recalling at will the smallest details of what he studied. During his years at Harrow, he memorized twelve hundred lines of Macaulay's *Lays of Ancient Rome* and won an award for reciting them without error. Later, at Sandhurst, Winston received some of the highest marks in his class for the study of history, particularly English history. And when he launched his program of self-education on the Indian frontier, he not only focused on the study of history, but also read so intently that decades later he was able to quote entire chapters of the Gibbon or Macaulay that he first encountered in those important months.

During his reading in India he also began to formulate a philosophy of history. He decided that men, exceptional men of character and vision, shape history by rising to the challenge of great events. As he said in his tribute to Lord Halifax, "The fortunes of mankind in its tremendous journeys are principally decided for good or ill–but mainly for good, for the path is upward–by its greatest men and its greatest episodes." [78] He concluded also that history has a great deal to do with the progress of "Christendom," that a moral order does govern in the affairs of men, that war is a natural and necessary condition of mankind, and that history teaches lessons that men ignore at their peril. "We cannot say 'the past is past,'" he insisted, "without surrendering the future."[79]

Churchill had a reverent regard for the power of history and he used it like a cannon when events demanded it. When the moment came for him to rally the spirit of sacrifice from an embattled people, Churchill knew from his study of the past and his own experience that men do not easily give their lives for governments or those who lead them. He was confident, though, that they would rise to victory if they could just see themselves as he did, in the light of their glorious history, their time-honored traditions, the destiny of their generation, and the future of their race.

> *Do not let us speak of darker days; let us speak rather of sterner days. These are not dark days; these are great days—the greatest days our country has ever lived; and we must all thank God that we have been allowed, each of us according to our stations, to play a part in making these days memorable in the history of our race.*[80]

And again:

> *This is no time to speak of the hopes of the future, or the broader world which lies beyond our struggles and our victory. We have to win that world for our children. We have to win it by our sacrifices. We have not won it yet.*[81]

Churchill knew that men are made to live in vital continuity with what precedes them and with what follows when they are gone. He understood that through history flow forces that touch every generation and that, when understood, may move them to "their finest hour."

REALISM

"The truth is incontrovertible. Panic may resent it;
ignorance may deride it; malice may destroy it, but
there it is." [82]

*A*s a rule, human beings try to avoid unpleasant truths.
We prefer the comfortable to the unsettling. We dislike
harsh facts for the same reason we dislike mirrors: they force
us to stare our problems in the face. Historians have long
known that civilizations in crisis take refuge in myth and fantasy because the sensual, escapist world of imagination
promises deliverance from the cold, disturbing world of reality.
But the deliverance is never genuine: it is only a temporary
distraction, not real hope. Hope springs instead from coura-
geously confronting the truth, no matter how bleak or costly
it may be.

In complaining about the age of appeasement, Churchill
once said, "No one in great authority had the wit, ascendancy
or detachment from public folly to declare these fundamental,
brutal facts to the electorate." [83] This touches one of the distin-
guishing marks of his style of leadership: he believed in the

necessity of squarely facing the most ugly realities. How refreshing this is in our media age when public relations experts are mistaken for leaders and when every unsightly blemish or untidy fact is carefully reworked, re-painted, or retired. Churchill would have none of it: "It is no use dealing with illusions and make-believes. We must look at the facts. The world ... is too dangerous for anyone to be able to afford to nurse illusions. We must look at realities." [84]

Churchill possessed an almost mystical confidence in knowing the facts and facing them honestly, whatever the offense, as a critical step toward ultimate triumph. In September of 1932, he warned the House of Commons of the Nazi movement and urged honesty in dealing with the public. "I would now say, 'Tell the truth to the British People.' They are a tough people, a robust people. They may be a bit offended at the moment, but if you have told them exactly what is going on you have insured yourself against complaints and reproaches which are very unpleasant when they come home on the morrow of some disillusion...." [85] Years later, as First Lord of the Admiralty, he told the House of Commons of a major naval defeat and reminded the members, "We do not at all underrate the power and malignity of our enemies. We are prepared to endure tribulation." [86] And when the defeats continued, his conclusion was near brutal in its frankness: "We shall suffer and we shall suffer continually, but by perseverance, and by taking measure on the largest scale, I feel no doubt that in the end we shall break their hearts." [87]

This resolve to engage the truth at any price granted Churchill some immensely important insights. As a careful observer who refused to change facts to fit his philosophy or bend reality to his imagination, he acquired shrewd insight into the ways of men and events. While others fashioned fantastic theories to explain what little they understood, Churchill recognized that history does not arrive in neat packages or move in defined channels. Time, chance, human nature–all play their role. Life is not black and white, events are stubborn and unruly, and men rarely follow precise patterns in their behavior. Understanding this gave Churchill the judgment to fashion policies suited to the fluid and uncertain nature of circumstances.

> *The world, nature, human beings, do not move like machines. The edges are never clear-cut, but always frayed. Nature never draws a line without smudging it. Conditions are so variable, episodes so unexpected, experiences so conflicting, that flexibility of judgment and a willingness to assume a somewhat humbler attitude towards external phenomena may well play their part in the equipment of a modern prime minister.*[88]

A "humbler attitude" meant caution in dealing with other human beings: "The high belief in the perfection of man is appropriate in a man of the cloth but not in a prime minister."[89] It also demanded an unnatural willingness to consider opposing views: "The more knowledge we possess of the opposite point of view the less puzzling it is to know what to do."[90] It enabled him to coolly calculate risk: "We realize that success cannot be guaranteed. There are no safe battles." And it made him even more impatient when empty posturing replaced informed action: "Peace will not be preserved by pious sentiments expressed in terms of platitudes or by official grimaces and diplomatic correctitude." Perhaps above all, it gave him a healthy sense of the absurd in the affairs of men: "The human story does not always unfold like a mathematical calculation on the principle that two and two make four. Sometimes in life they make five or minus three; and sometimes the blackboard topples down in the middle of the sum and leaves the class in disorder and the pedagogue with a black eye."

Facing ugly truth is not easy. Often the toughest battle a leader will face is the one against his own reticence to see things as they really are. It requires uncommon courage and very few have the character to deal with such stark reality. But when the truth is known, the worst is over and the benefits are a clearer vision and the wisdom of a "humbler attitude," without which leaders cannot move beyond despair to a brighter day of victory.

HUMOR

"In my belief, you cannot deal with the most serious things in the world unless you also understand the most amusing." [91]

an," said English essayist William Hazlitt, in *The English Comic Writers*, "is the only animal that laughs and weeps: for he is the only animal that is struck by the difference between what things are and what they ought to be." [92] If this is true, then genuine humor arises from something akin to a largeness of soul, an inner breadth so all-encompassing as to embrace both the commonplace and the ideal, both life's ugliness and its stunning beauty, both the normal and the absurd. Such is the soul of great leadership, and such was the soul of Winston Churchill.

Wit, which Webster defines as "the ability to relate seemingly disparate things so as to illuminate or amuse," flowed effortlessly from Churchill. His was not the humor of the comedian, that of the joke or the anecdote. Instead, he combined a non-conformist's perspective with an awe-inspiring command of language to produce an often disarming and sometimes shattering effect that always extended his meaning.

Once when visiting the White House, Churchill emerged from his daily bath just as President Roosevelt was wheeled into his room. Roosevelt was deeply embarrassed and apologized profusely while beating a hasty retreat. Astutely, Churchill seized the moment for a larger cause. Holding up a detaining hand, he solemnly proclaimed, "The Prime Minister of Great Britain has nothing to hide from the President of the United States." When the cliché "familiarity breeds contempt" was once used in an argument against him, he thundered, "I would like to remind you that without a degree of familiarity we could not breed anything."[93] When *Pygmalion* was beginning at His Majesty's Theatre, George Bernard Shaw wired Winston: "Am reserving two tickets for you for my premiere. Come and bring a friend–if you have one." Churchill, who could give as good as he got, wired Shaw back: "Impossible to be present for the first performance. Will attend the second–if there is one."[94]

But Churchill's wit could be quite acidic, as well. He was unwilling to suffer fools, had a fiery temper, and was not adverse to making "a few remarks of a general character, mostly beginning with the earlier letters of the alphabet."[95] He said of John Foster Dulles that he was "dull, duller, Dulles." He called Clement Attlee a "sheep in sheep's clothing" and "a modest man with much to be modest about." Lady Astor, a constant thorn in Churchill's side, once said in exasperation, "Winston, if I were your wife I'd put poison in your coffee." He replied without hesitation, "Nancy, if I were your husband, I'd drink it." To another woman who said that she liked neither his politics nor the new mustache he was sporting, he retorted, "Madam, I see no earthly reason why you should come into contact with either."[96] And in a manner typical of his style, he fired a broadside against one despised breed by simply defining them for ages to come. "A fanatic," he jibed, "is one who can't change his mind and won't change the subject."[97]

He was not a stone-faced wit, though, and he enjoyed the occasion of a laugh as much as anyone. Friends noted that he had a habit of "throwing back his head and laughing heartily."[98] His fellow members of Parliament learned to look for the signs that a classic "Churchillism" was on its way:

> *One always knew it was coming. His own laughter began somewhere in the region of his feet. Then a leg would twitch; the bubble of mirth was slowly rising through the body. The stomach would swell; a shoulder heave. By this time, the audience would also be convulsed, although it had no idea what the joke was going to be. Meanwhile, the bubble had ascended a little further and had reached the face; the lips were as mobile and expressive as a baby's. The rich, stumbling voice would become even more hesitant. And finally there would be the explosion, the triumphant sentence of ridicule.*[99]

Yet, he took wit seriously, even as he did language and the spoken word. His secretary recorded that once while touring slums, he remarked, "Fancy living in one of these streets, never seeing anything beautiful, never eating anything savoury, *never saying anything clever.*"[100] Churchill's wit is similar to that found in many great leaders. It sprang from a yearning to find acceptance, certainly, but it also found its origin in a kind of compassion, in a genuine affection and a hope of touching more than the mind with the power of truth. Herbert Elliston, editor of the *Washington Post*, perhaps better than anyone understood the impact of Churchill's wit and, through it, the wit required of leaders in difficult times.

Churchill will live if only in his witticisms. And these will be the stock of conversation in all countries for a long time to come. They are as much a revelation of character as anything he said or did–as much, also, of an influence among men. In wartime they passed by word of mouth all over the world wherever men were struggling with the aggressor and planning a new life in liberty. They lightened the burdens of the dispirited and were quoted as the words of a champion. [101]

CHARACTER

"Never give in, never give in, never, never, never, never–in nothing, great or small, large or petty– never give in except to convictions of honor and good sense." [102]

 Winston Churchill's philosophy was "never give in." And yet...his father, a man so remote that he was rarely sure of his son's age, ended his life in diseased insanity. His mother was rumored to be a notorious adulteress who lived for her own pleasure and paid little attention to her son until he became famous.

From the moment of birth, he was astonishingly sickly and weak. In his childhood he endured "cold after cold" and contracted any disease he was near. When he was eleven, he almost died of pneumonia, an ailment that visited him with regularity throughout his life. He was particularly prone to rashes, boils, and hives, and friends teased him about the silk underwear that he wore to prevent maddening skin irritations. In the last decades of his life, he suffered numerous strokes. One historian wrote that his death from one illness or another was expected almost every year of his life.

He was small, too. Even at eighteen years of age he was a mere five feet, six inches tall and his hairless chest measured only thirty-one inches, expanding a paltry two inches with a full breath. He would never be taller than five feet, seven inches. [103] All his life people were deceived by the way his oversized shoulders made him look taller in photographs and they tortured him by callously reminding him of how short he really was.

He also was born with a troubling speech impediment. Like his father before him, he had difficulty pronouncing the letter *s*. Some called it a stammer and others a lisp, but political opponents doted on it mercilessly and, much to his frustration, he never fully conquered it.

In addition he was notoriously accident prone. It was perfectly in keeping with his manner that he went bike riding and ended up with a concussion, played tag and ended up unconscious for three days, climbed out of a boat and damaged his shoulder so badly he was unable to raise his arm for the rest of his life, and visited New York only to be struck by a taxi going over thirty miles an hour. He forgot, he said later, that traffic in America flows in the opposite direction from that in England. The taxi blind-sided him, mangled him underneath, and threw him out onto the busy Manhattan thoroughfare. He was more than a year in healing.

As soon as Winston knew what money was, he spent it with astonishing excess. He was in debt most of his life. He lost a fortune in the Wall Street stock market crash of 1929 and would have been left completely bankrupt had American financier Bernard Baruch not intervened. For long periods of time his writing was motivated largely by a need to stay ahead of bills. Without the help of friends, he probably would have lost Chartwell, his beloved home.

Politically, Churchill's star fell and rose again many times. He lost his first election, but then won later after gaining fame in South Africa. He became one of the youngest cabinet members in British history before World War I, but following the disastrous defeat in the Dardanelles, for which he was blamed, he was dismissed from the Admiralty. During most of the 1930's he was in political exile, deserted even by his friends. With the onset of World War II, he was again placed in the Admiralty and soon after became Prime Minister. However, at the conclusion of the War, the British people voted him out of office, only to vote him in again six years later. In his time, he lost more elections than any other British politician.

His political misfortunes contributed to the agonizing bouts of depression he suffered throughout his life. He called them "my Black Dog." Like many great leaders before him–Luther and Lincoln for example–he lived much of his life from deep within a cavernous blackness. His depressions drove him to ponder suicide. He told friends that he feared standing near the edge of the platform at a train station or sleeping near a balcony. "I've no desire to quit this world, but thoughts, desperate thoughts, come into the head." [104] In old age he gloomily told his children, "I have achieved a great deal to achieve nothing in the end." [105]

In 1921, his youngest child, Marigold, died at the age of two. The infant, whom her father lovingly nicknamed "Duckadilly," caught a cold that advanced into septicemia. When the little girl died, her mother shrieked "like an animal in mortal pain." Winston was devastated. "Poor lamb," he wrote months later, "it is a gaping wound, whenever one touches it and removes the bandages and plasters of daily life." [106]

His other children were, save one, troubled. His son Randolph was a violent drunk whose life was marred by scandals, divorces and "infirmity of purpose." [107] Sarah, who chose acting as a career against her father's wishes, was also given to drunkenness and jumped in and out of relationships with regularity but with little happiness. Diana shared her father's "Black Dog" depressions. She committed suicide at the age of 54. Only Mary, Winston's youngest, often called by friends "wise and good," embodied both her mother's prudence and her father's character.

His was not a life easy or charmed. He was, perhaps above all, completely human. Nevertheless, believing that life has purpose and that an "order" exists, he wrote, "Let us reconcile ourselves to our destinies, such as they must be in this world of space and time. Let us treasure our joys but not bewail our sorrows. The glory of light cannot exist without its shadows. Life is a whole, and good and ill must be taken together." [108]

Never give in, never give in, never, never, never, never...

Self-Examination

"The final tribute is our own conscience." [109]

One of the most endearing and valuable traits a leader can possess is an attitude of genuine self-criticism. A sense of humility and lightheartedness about oneself that springs from honest self-examination is of inestimable value. It allows leaders to see the world as it is by burning off the fog of self-importance. The tragedy of many leaders is that they live in an artificial environment, insulated from the natural corrections of life. They begin to believe their own press releases. They cease to question themselves or heed advice. In short, they become dangerous. They no longer inspire meaningful change because they are unwilling to change themselves.

The initial impression people gained from encounters with Winston Churchill was not one of humility. Like many leaders, he was bold, often pushy, and exuded an aura of power and confidence. Yet, behind the public persona, Churchill was a man given to long bouts with a kind of depression that brought him face to face with his own weaknesses. He knew only too well his dark side, his insecurities, his inner deformities. His "Black Dog" depressions showed him a disconcerting mirror image of who he really was. The strength of Churchill, though, was that he refused to forget what he saw in these dark nights of the soul. He could have denied it or sought some soothing escape from it. Instead, he learned from it and let it make him a better man.

From the battlefront, Churchill once wrote his wife, "Sometimes also I think I would not mind stopping living very much. I am so devoured by egoism that I would like to have another soul in another world and meet you in another setting." [110] This statement is typical of him. Others might think him self-centered and egotistical; he knew it best of all and hated it more than anyone else could. But the central point is that he recognized it, that he had peered sufficiently into himself to know. Even his public admissions of wrongdoing showed that he took the time to consider the implications of his actions. In a speech to the House of Commons on June 25, 1941, he said, "I do not think any expression of scorn or severity which I have heard used by our critics has come anywhere near the language I have been myself accustomed to use, not only orally, but in a stream of written minutes. In fact, I wonder that a great many of my colleagues are on speaking terms with me." [111]

Churchill also exhibited that rare quality of self-effacing humor that grows from honest self-examination. It prompted some of his greatest and most memorable lines. When a lady asked him if it did not thrill him to realize that his speeches always brought overflow audiences, he responded, "It is quite flattering ... but whenever I feel this way I always remember that if instead of making a political speech I was being hanged, the crowd would be twice as big." [112] Of meeting a member of the royal family, he wrote, "I realized that I must be on my best behavior–punctual, subdued, reserved–in short, display all the qualities with which I am least endowed."[113] When he spoke in Paris after the liberation of France, he said, "Be on your guard! I am going to speak in French–a formidable undertaking and one which will put great demands upon your friendship for Great Britain."[114] And in a 1945 speech in the Commons, he quipped, "If I am accused of this mistake, I can only say with Mr. Clemenceau on a celebrated occasion: 'Perhaps I have made a number of other mistakes of which you have not heard.'"[115]

One of the most public failures of Churchill's life forced him to painfully evaluate and confess his mistakes. In 1924, Prime Minister Stanley Baldwin appointed him the Chancellor of the Exchequer, England's chief financial officer. Churchill had never been good with math or what he called "the dismal bog of sums."[116] While in office, he remarked, "The higher mind has no need to concern itself with the meticulous regimentation of figures."[117] This was not the attitude toward "figures" the British public wanted from its Lord of the Treasury. Nevertheless, Churchill marched confidently on, and took the major step of returning Britain to the gold standard. The disastrous result was hyperinflation, unemployment, and the closing of businesses essential to the national life. The country was outraged. Churchill at first bristled, but later admitted, "Everyone said I was the worst Chancellor of the Exchequer that ever was, and now I am inclined to agree with them."[118] True to form, he faced the truth about himself and held it aloft for all to see.

On an occasion when Churchill was giving advice to his commanders during war, he said:

> *Don't be careless about yourselves–on the other*
> *hand not too careful. Live well but do not*
> *flaunt it. Laugh a little and teach your men to*

*laugh–get good humor under fire–war is a
game that's played with a smile. If you can't
smile, grin. If you can't grin, keep out of the way
till you can.*[119]

These words say a great deal about his character and also
about why historians have a difficult time pinning Churchill
down. He believed in destiny but also in not caring for oneself
"too much." He took war very seriously but could call it a game.
He knew he had a mission, but wanted to fulfill it with a smile.
He possessed balance and a holistic, honest world view that
incorporated all life's offerings. He could hold seeming oppo-
sites in a dynamic tension because he faced the truth about
himself, found it complex, came to terms with it, and moved
forward determined make his mark–but to do it with a smile.
It is possible only for those who live the self-examined life.

THE MASTERY OF SELF

"We are all worms, but I intend to be a glowworm." [120]

The pages of history are filled with people who achieved greatness by prevailing over disadvantage and deformity. In the now familiar stories, stutterers became great orators, cripples became mighty athletes, men born to squalor ascended to great wealth, and women without education served mankind with genius. Touching and inspiring, these legends are retold whenever the fires of determination require stoking. In each of these stories, though, a critical decision had to be made; men can change their circumstances. Biology and sociology need not be destiny. Through will, concentration, sacrifice, and patience, adversity can be mastered. In fact, so many esteemed men and women have achieved their success by conquering obstacles that one wonders if real greatness is possible apart from staggering difficulties. The lesson of history seems clear: character hewn through struggle is the price of true greatness.

If this is true, then the magnificence of Churchill is easily explained. So numerous and crushing were his early difficulties,

so understandable his opportunities for failure, that the honor
he commands is only magnified when men learn of his trials.
He was born a small, sickly child with a maddening lisp.
Physically weak and accident prone, he was a favorite target of
his schoolmates, so he coped by insulating himself in a solitary
world of fantasy. The difficulty of those years coupled with his
own rebelliousness robbed him of the education he should
have had and left him academically far behind his peers. This
marked him with an abiding sense of intellectual inferiority.
His mother worried that he would never rise above medioc-
rity and his father never stopped talking about his own bitter
disappointment over his disturbing son.

Lord Randolph's venom nearly cursed Winston with self-
hatred and failure. A crumbling political career and eroding
sanity left him a broken, bitter man and Winston became the
object of his poison. Even late in life, Winston remembered
clearly the angry darts that once pierced his soul: "Bottom of
the school! Never passed any examination, except into the cavalry. Wrote me stilted letters. I could not see how you would
make your living on the little I could leave you and Jack, and
that only after your mother. I once thought of the bar for you,
but you were not clever enough." [121] Typically, when Winston's
first book met with wide acclaim, his father's disapproval
"destroyed all the pleasure that I had hoped to get from the
book," leaving only "shame that such an impertinence should
be presented to the public." [122]

Lord Randolph concluded, "You will be a wastrel" of
"slovenly, shiftless habits." But Winston had two qualities that
saved him from this fate and set him on a road of ambitious
self-improvement. First, he was brutally honest in assessing
his own weaknesses. He knew himself well and told his
mother, for example, "Being in many ways a coward–and particularly at school–there is no ambition I cherish so keenly as

to gain a reputation for personal courage." [123] Repeatedly, in Churchill's writings and public pronouncements, one finds a rare humility and truthfulness, an almost jovial self-criticism in regard to his own characteristics. It is endearing, but more importantly it moved him to strive for change. The second quality that saved Winston from his father's evil script was an astounding ability to exert himself against his own nature, to force himself to go beyond what by all accounts he was destined to be.

This volcanic determination, this almost brutal self-command, is the engine of Churchill's greatness. Though his body type and personality inherently gravitated toward the comfortable and unchallenging, some force within him–perhaps his overwhelming sense of destiny–enabled him to drive his whole being against nature to become the man he wanted to be. True, he lived in the Victorian era, when the ideal of mastering one's fate, the images of the rags-to-riches story, and the nearly patriotic call to self-improvement together formed a cult of achievement. But there was still something more in Churchill, something titanic, that moved him to attack obstacles with a focus borne of desperation and ambition. One historian has described it well: "Acutely aware of his deficiencies, he started to re-create himself in preparation for the life he wanted. His determination was worthy of the young Napoleon himself." [124]

He saw that the public man he intended to be could never succeed without skill as an orator. So, he rehearsed tirelessly, and eventually melded his lisp, his stage-fright, his incredible memory, and his passion for the English language into a potent weapon. In like manner, he found himself feeling quite inferior to his university-trained fellow Army officers. It would not do. Instantly, the torrid afternoons of the Indian hot season were transformed into five hours of intense reading and research.

Through this Churchill emerged as a learned man. Similarly, whenever he was in battle, though by nature a safety-seeking coward, Winston thrust himself into the thickest fighting, often placing himself in such peril that other soldiers pleaded with him to find cover. He was decorated for his bravery, but his greatest reward was unseen, for secretly he knew he had driven himself against his grain to be a soldier worthy of his vision.

Other weaknesses and deficiencies also were conquered, but it almost does not matter which ones they were. Having declared war on anything in him that resisted his vision, he knew his drive could overcome even his own personality and biology. In recent decades, many have spoken of Churchill's "indomitable will," but this force was first summoned in the greatest of all his battles—the battle for mastery over himself.

COMPASSION

"One should be just before one is generous." [125]

There is a difference between pity and compassion. Pity is an entirely emotional response of sorrow for another's ill-fortune. It is feeling not necessarily accompanied by action. Compassion, on the other hand, moves people to action. It is more than sympathizing, more than sharing another's feelings. Compassion is the potent combination of genuine empathy with fiery determination to create change. Throughout history, pity has been the luxury of every age, but compassion marks only strong and noble societies rooted in something beyond material gain and sensual indulgence. The same is true of leaders.

Winston Churchill is remembered for many things, but compassion is seldom one of them. Few know that he considered it one of his life's purposes to bring an end to suffering and that he was a leading social reformer in his day. This is unfortunate, for it says a great deal about the compassion that motivated Churchill in his life of public service. Great leaders must care for those they lead and be moved by their suffering, otherwise they degenerate into cynicism and manipulation. Often, like Churchill, they must send thousands to their deaths with steely resolve, but when they cannot feel the loss–when they cannot weep with compassion, as Churchill wept when viewing his dead countrymen–they no longer possess the humanity necessary for greatness.

Churchill's compassionate nature is exemplified best in his battle against the poverty of the Edwardian era. Through his nanny, Mrs. Everest, he first came into contact with what were called the "lower classes," and experienced the way most of the people in Great Britain lived. It did not impact him initially, but later, when he read studies of the desperate poverty in England at the time, he recalled her humble circumstances and the lessons of caring and responsibility she taught. Already swept up in Lloyd George's great reform movement, Churchill determined that the moment had come for the lot of the poor to change. More than that, he determined that he was the man to make it happen.

Churchill approached the problems of the poor with a burning sense of mission. A friend who visited him during the infancy of his cause wrote, "Winston swept me off to his cousin's house and I lay on the bed while he dressed and marched around the room, gesticulating and impetuous, pouring out all his hopes and plans and ambitions. He is full of the poor, whom he has just discovered. He thinks he is called by providence to do something for them. 'Why have I been kept safe to within a hair's breadth of death,' he asked, 'except to do something like this?'" [126]

The sweep of the reforms Churchill championed are as astonishing today as they were then. With Clementine's encouragement–and critical of "our unbridled Imperialists who have no thought but to pile up armaments, taxation, and territory"–he initiated an excess-profits tax, established labor exchanges, instituted minimum standards for sweatshops, prevented industrial exploitation of children, and began a system of national insurance.[127] Most of this was accomplished through the "People's Budget" of 1909 which Churchill and Lloyd George drafted together won national acclaim as its leading advocate.

Some scholars speak of him as the "Father of the Modern Welfare State," but Churchill was never the radical socialist he is portrayed to be. He said his ideal political party was one "free at once from the sordid selfishness and callousness of Toryism on the one hand and the blind appetites of the Radical masses on the other."[128] In his later career, he vehemently opposed the Labour party's cradle-to-grave welfare legislation. Typically, he believed socialism was "contrary to human nature," that it was the "philosophy of failure, the creed of ignorance and the gospel of envy."[129] He was no radical, but he was in favor of serving compassionate ends with the power of government. Years after his reform efforts began, he wrote "When I think of the fate of poor old women, so many of whom have no one to look after them and nothing to live on at the end of their lives, I am glad to have had a hand in all that structure of pensions and insurance which no other country can rival and which is especially a help to them."[130]

His deep compassion also led him into one of the darkest periods of his life. When he became Home Secretary in 1910, his responsibilities included reviewing the records of prisoners condemned to death. Churchill had experienced prison conditions under the Boers in South Africa and it made a lasting impression. "Looking back on those days," he wrote, "I have always felt the keenest pity for prisoners and captives. What it must mean for any man, especially an educated man, to be confined for years in a modern convict prison strains my imagination. Each day exactly like the one before, with the barren ashes of wasted life behind, and all the long years of bondage stretching out ahead." [131] Immersed in the details of these tragic lives day after day, he began to slip into a deep "Black Dog" depression. Years later, he told his doctor, Lord Moran, "For two or three years the light faded from the picture. I did my work. I sat in the House of Commons, but black depression settled on me." [132] Only the tender attention of Clementine kept him from losing himself completely.

It is not uncharacteristic of him that when a fund was suggested in his honor in 1944, he refused, but added, "If, however, when I am dead people think of commemorating my services, I should like to think that a park was made for the children of London's poor on the south bank of the Thames, where they have suffered so grimly from the Hun." [133] Public figures in Churchill's age made much of expressing pity, not a difficult sentiment in those desperate times. But compassion moved Churchill to the kind of action that brought meaningful change to the lives of people, from aged women to the children of the Blitz. This is the soul of extraordinary leadership–meaningful action powered by heartfelt devotion to the needs of others.

HOME

*"We shape our dwellings and afterwards our
dwellings shape us."* [134]

hen his work is done, or at least at a pause, what a
leader needs most is a place of safety, a place where
he can renew his vision and gain strength for the next battle.
This place is called home. Here, insulated from the press of life
and nurtured by family and the familiar, his burden may be
no lighter but at least he will have a chance to reclaim the reason he bears it. He will begin to see again what he cannot see
in the fray of his calling. He may read an inspiring passage
from a beloved book or kiss the forehead of the next generation or draw sustenance from the hearts of those who believe
in him–but whatever his antidote, he will gain what he needs
to go out once more with determination and purpose.

For Winston Churchill, the place for reclaiming what life
stripped away was Chartwell, a rather odd conglomeration of
structures on the Kentish weald, some of it dating back to
Henry VII and some of it modern. For Churchill, it was an
"earthly paradise." [135] Though he was not unfamiliar with

king's palaces and the grand estates of the English nobility–
he was born in the awe-inspiring Blenheim Palace, ancestral
home of the Dukes of Marlborough–humble Chartwell was
his beloved home. To celebrate his preference, he delighted in
quoting a poem by Alexander Pope called *Upon the Duke of
Marlborough's House at Woodstock.*

> *See, Sir, here's the grand approach,*
> *This way is for his Grace's coach;*
> *There lies the bridge, and here's the clock;*
> *Observe the lion and the cock,*
> *The spacious court, the colonnade,*
> *And mark how wide the hall is made!*
> *The chimneys are so well design'd*
> *They never smoke in any wind.*
> *This gallery's contrived for walking,*
> *The windows to retire and talk in;*
> *The council-chamber for debate,*
> *And all the rest are rooms of state,*
> *Thanks, Sir, cried I, 'tis very fine,*
> *but where d'ye sleep, or where d'ye dine?*
> *I find by all you have been telling*
> *That 'tis a house, but not a dwelling.*[136]

Churchill bought Chartwell in 1924 with earnings from
The World Crisis and a partial inheritance. Clementine hated
the monstrosity, but Winston was beside himself with joy. He
had found a home: land of his own, a piece of England. He
reveled in it. Clementine saw only dirt and boards and rooms
that required cleaning. Winston saw an estate, a legacy, the
stately domain of a nobleman and his family. He announced,
"A day away from Chartwell is a day wasted," and he eagerly
began planning how he would transform the house and the

land to fit his dreams. It was the perfect outlet for his renaissance energies.

> *I lived mainly at Chartwell where I had much
> to amuse me. I built with my own hands a large
> part of the cottages and extensive kitchen-
> garden walls, and made all kinds of rockeries
> and waterworks and a large swimming pool
> which was filtered to limpidity and could be
> heated to supplement our fickle sunshine. Thus
> I never had a dull or idle moment from morning
> to midnight, and with my happy family around
> me dwelt at peace within my habitation.*[137]

For a short while, Churchill had visions of himself as a gentleman farmer and made the place thick with animals. A guest at Chartwell was likely to come across a marmalade cat, Carolina ducks, swans, polo ponies, Canada geese, cygnets, any number or variety of dogs, lambs, golden orfe, sheldrakes, chickens, or pigs. But Churchill was no farmer: animals died of various diseases–or, like one billy goat, because they butted their owner. Plans to live off the land were scrapped, but that didn't stop Churchill from imagining himself a man of the soil.

Because Churchill loved Chartwell so much, he delighted in welcoming his friends there. As he told his friend Eddie Marsh, "You could rest comfortably here…just vegetate as I do."[138] The guest list was lengthy and included such notables as Charlie Chaplin, T. E. Lawrence ("Lawrence of Arabia"), and Harry Truman, and when friends dined at Chartwell there was sure to be lively conversation, glorious food, heated debate, and even lengthy recitations of poetry or the retelling of an ancient battle with tableware serving as weaponry. Churchill delighted in the buzzing activity, but in time the tone of his gatherings changed. With the rise of Nazi Germany and the astonishing weakness of the British government in the 1930's, Chartwell became "a little Foreign Office." [139] Churchill's network of experts and supporters often could be found meeting there late into the night like a shadow cabinet. Discussions might range from the output of German munitions factories, to the problems of the Spitfire, to the latest debates in Parliament. During this time, a friend noted, "Winston is happy at Chartwell, as happy as he can be when the world has gone all wrong."

One has only to hear the many references to land in Churchill's speeches to know how deeply Chartwell affected him. Chartwell was home, but it was also earth and England and belonging and place. It is no wonder that he once said with weepy emotion, "I love the place." [140]

POETRY OF LIFE

"Expert knowledge, however indispensable, is no substitute for a generous and comprehending outlook upon a human story with all its sadness—with all its unquenchable hope." [141]

There is a tendency among people in positions of responsibility to lose sight of the emotions and experiences that give meaning to the very idea of leadership. Long experience with the tough issues of life leaves its mark and it is easy to give in to a hardened view of the world. When this happens, though, the leader diminishes himself. He may be skillful and competent, but he has lost the ability to inspire and create. The difficult challenge is to endure the jarring battles of life without letting go of the feeling and innocent wonder that make those battles worthwhile.

Winston Churchill was saved from many of the pitfalls of leadership because he was an absolutely unapologetic romantic. Except for his periods of depression, he seemed to ever have in view a cheery, ideal world of romance and beauty. He was a fiery realist but he also believed that imagination, tenderness, and laughter have their place. "We want a lot of engineers in the world," he said, "but we do not want a world of engineers." [142]

Anything but an engineer, Churchill was a romantic of the most emotional and tearful kind. "I've always been blubbery," he confessed. William Manchester suggests that his "tears flowed at the mention of gallantry in battle, the thought of 'invincible knights in olden days,' victims of anti-Semitism, Canadian loyalty to the Empire, the death of George VI, Elizabeth II's kindness toward him, or the name of Franklin Roosevelt–'the best friend Britain ever had.'" [143] Observers who stood close enough saw that he wept through many of his speeches, during visits to bomb damage in London, and when lists of battle casualties crossed his desk. But he wept over much more mundane things as well. He loved to watch movies, and during a showing of *Never Take No for an Answer*, a movie about a little boy and a dying donkey, Churchill became undone. "Oh, the donkey's dead!" he sobbed. "No, no, Prime Minister, she's alive," consoled his staff members. "If the donkey dies, I shan't stay. I shall go out," Churchill tearfully insisted. [144]

Ironically, his profuse tears gave rise to his reputation for drunkenness, a reputation he encouraged himself. Churchill was embarrassed by his emotionalism and thought it unmanly. Since he lived at a time when an ability to hold alcohol was prized, he thought it better to blame his emotionalism on drink. In reality he drank very little. True, he started each day with a scotch and soda, but that one drink lasted until noon and the amount of alcohol he consumed in a day was actually very small. One observer confided, "I've never seen anyone make a double brandy last as long as Sir Winston." [145] As he wrote in *My Early Life*, "I had been brought up and trained to have the utmost contempt for people who got drunk." [146] Once when he asked his friend, Frederick Lindemann, to compute how many boxcars could be filled by the champagne he had consumed, "the Prof" disappointed Churchill by saying, "Only part of one." [147]

That Churchill was both a romantic and an individualist made for some touching and amusing moments. When a wartime conference at Chequers took a 3 a.m. smoking break, someone found a piano and began playing "The Blue Danube." The assembled generals and cabinet officials were astonished when the Prime Minister "all alone, started waltzing dreamily around the floor." [148] Household staff at Chartwell were sometimes alarmed to hear yelling and screaming coming from one of the rooms. In time they learned not to be concerned: it was Churchill, during one of his lengthy baths, lost in reliving a speech or battle, or moving himself to tears with poetry or the memory of a departed friend.

He was unreservedly sentimental. His love for animals, for example, bordered on the absurd. He routinely called Chartwell from London to check on dying goldfish, cried at the death of a cat, picked up dead animals on the side of the road, ordered his staff to report to him on the "liberation" of a lady bug, and summoned the fish in the Chartwell ponds each by name for their supper. His wife once had a Chartwell goose cooked for dinner. Winston couldn't bring himself to even carve the cooked bird. Turning to his wife, he said, "You carve him, Clemmie. He was a friend of mine." [149] His favorite animal was Rufus, a poodle, who slept, ate, and had regular discourse with him. When a maid let him off his leash and the little dog was killed, Churchill never spoke to the poor woman again.

But Churchill was stirred by noble themes as well. He could speak movingly of the British empire, Christendom, the monarchy, war, and motherhood, because each of these struck a deep chord in his own soul. In the same way, poetry had a hypnotic effect on him. He was transported by Rupert Brooke, Henry Wadsworth Longfellow, and especially Rudyard Kipling. In 1953, he movingly quoted all thirty-four lines of Longfellow's "King Robert of Sicily," a poem he had committed to memory fifty years earlier. He was captivated by the images of epic poetry and in his later years his greatest pleasure was for one of his children to read to him the poetic accounts of ages past.

Churchill refused to insulate himself from life. Instead, he charged into it. His strength as a statesman was due in part to the romantic passion and tenderness he nurtured in himself. He allowed himself to be stirred, gave himself to the elevation that came from caring, and refused to insulate himself from the inconvenience of his emotions. He reached people of widely differing experience because he was able to feel, and feel deeply, for he knew that emotional sterility is death to great leadership.

REST

"A change is as good as a rest." [150]

His hobbies included acting, singing, butterfly collecting, chess, theater, fencing, gardening, gymnastics, painting, polo, horseback riding, squash, swimming, reading, bridge, bezique, gin rummy, shooting, fishing, golf, hunting, horse racing, flying, military games, bricklaying, gambling, music, landscaping, travel, and farming. Was he a man of leisure?

Not exactly. This same man fought in four wars, served in his nation's parliament over a period of sixty-three years, led his country as prime minister for almost ten years, wrote 50 books, published hundreds of articles, gave thousands of speeches, reared four children, and worked to keep a marriage intact for over fifty-five years. The man was Winston Churchill, and he knew something about stress. But he also knew about rest.

Churchill was a man of exceptional intensity and determination. His aggressive style of leadership and his energetic passion for life could have depleted him long before he reached his most productive years. But he learned early a lesson some leaders never master: the greater the capacity for concentration and hard work, the greater the tendency toward exhaustion and burnout. Left unchecked, the very qualities that make a man successful are the ones that can lead him blindly into a fruitless, lethargic abyss of self-destruction.

From hard experience, Churchill knew how easy it is for a leader to deceive himself. It begins when the leader starts treating his work like a holy crusade, worthy of sacrificing all. Having accepted this lie, he then begins to believe that the work is so important that others should not be entrusted with it: only he can do it right. This is the trap, though, and soon, noticing that his work hours are less and less productive, he compensates by working longer and harder. The trap is sprung and the suicidal spiral begins. What he has failed to see is that his own proud and unceasing devotion to work is dulling his faculties. He needs a rest, but he cannot get off the fast-moving train that he himself has sent hurtling down the tracks.

Churchill saw this dynamic in himself and observed it in his closest colleagues. He believed he had the answer to it. In an article entitled simply *Hobbies*, first published in 1932, Churchill explained his understanding of how work takes its toll and how the damage can be undone.

> *A man can wear out a particular part of his mind by continually using it and tiring it, just in the same way as he can wear out the elbows of his coat. There is, however, this difference between the living cells of the brain and inanimate articles: one cannot mend the frayed elbows of a coat by rubbing the sleeves or shoulders; but the tired parts of the mind can be rested and strengthened not merely by rest, but by using other parts. It is not enough merely*

> *to switch off the lights which play upon the*
> *main and ordinary field of interest; a new field*
> *of interest must be illuminated.* [151]

Change, he had discovered, was the "master key." He had tried simple rest but found that it did not bring the needed refreshing. "It is no use saying to the tired 'mental muscles'– if one may coin such an expression–'I will give you a good rest,' 'I will go for a long walk,' or 'I will lie down and think of nothing.' The mind keeps busy just the same. If it has been weighing and measuring, it goes on weighing and measuring. If it has been worrying, it goes on worrying. It is only when new cells are called into activity, when new stars become the lords of the ascendant, that relief, repose, refreshment are afforded." [152] And the simplest source of this invigorating change, in Churchill's opinion, was a hobby. "The cultivation of a hobby and new forms of interest is therefore a policy of first importance to a public man." [153]

So the hobby had to be chosen carefully. First, it must be enjoyable: "It is no use doing what you like, you must like what you do." [154] Second, one had to distinguish between a beneficial distraction on the one hand and mere activity on the other.

> *As for the unfortunate people who can com-*
> *mand everything they want, who can gratify*
> *every caprice and lay their hands on almost*
> *every object of desire–for them a new pleasure,*
> *a new excitement is only an additional satia-*
> *tion. In vain they rush frantically round from*
> *place to place, trying to escape from avenging*
> *boredom by mere clatter and motion. For them*
> *discipline in one form or another is the most*
> *hopeful path.* [155]

Finally, the hobby should include mental and physical exertion together: "To restore psychic equilibrium we should call into use those parts of the mind which direct both eye and hand." [156] His advice? "Choose well, choose wisely, and choose one." [157]

Churchill possessed the humility to see what many leaders ignore in their arrogance. He knew he was not invincible, not inexhaustible, so he developed the discipline of rest, of taking time from the battle to sharpen his sword. The legendary sharpness of his mind and endurance of his body were enhanced by his belief that a change is indeed as good as a rest, and that the best work is done by those who know when to stop working. Churchill did, and his life was richer, more productive, and more enjoyable for his wisdom.

THE WRITTEN WORD

"Thus I got into my bones the essential structure of the ordinary British sentence–which is a noble thing." [158]

He is known to the public as a politician and a war leader, yet more of his words have been put in print than those of Charles Dickens and Sir Walter Scott combined. He published fifty books, over eight hundred articles, three short stories, and one hundred and fifty pamphlets. He also wrote a novel, a film script, and contributed sections to eighty-three other works. Not to be excluded are the notes he wrote for a series of jigsaw puzzles and the fifty long- and short-play records to his credit. In 1953 he was awarded the Nobel Prize for literature, only the seventh Briton in history to receive the honor. His name was Winston Churchill, and his love affair with words and their meaning was the very lifeblood of his powerful kind of leadership.

This love affair probably began at Harrow when Churchill studied under a Mr. Somerwell. The "cleverer boys," as Winston styled them, were charged with learning Latin and Greek. It was Mr. Somerwell's task to teach "the stupidest boys the most disregarded thing–namely, to write mere English. He knew how to do it. He taught it as no one else has ever taught it."[159] Churchill remained in Somerwell's care three terms longer than the other boys, presumably because of his low grades and so, as he wrote, "I had three times as much of it. I learned it thoroughly."[160]

He apparently did, but it wasn't until his early twenties, when he began his voracious reading program, that he discovered a beauty in language beyond grammar alone. During his long hours of reading in India, he not only completed all of Bartlett's *Familiar Quotations* and memorized much of it, but he also devoured Gibbon and Macaulay for weeks on end. Their style was a revelation to him: "Macaulay is easier reading than Gibbon and in quite a different style. Macaulay crisp and forcible, Gibbon stately and impressive. Both are fascinating and show what a fine language English is since it can be pleasing in styles so different." The construction of Churchill's literary style was underway.

> *I began to see that writing, especially narrative, was not only an affair of sentences, but of paragraphs. Indeed I thought the paragraph no less important than the sentence. Macaulay is a master of paragraphing. Just as the sentence contains one idea in all its fullness, so the paragraphs must fit on to one another like the automatic couplings of railway carriages.*[161]

Armed with the lessons of these masters, he evolved an approach of his own in which he "affected the style of Macaulay and Gibbon, the staccato antitheses of the former and the rolling sentences and genitival endings of the latter; and I stuck in a bit of my own from time to time."[162]

The part that was his came from the wonder of an unfolding world of language. In her *Winston Churchill as I Knew Him*, Violet Asquith recounted how she read to Churchill some famous lines of poetry by Keats. "Later on he asked me whether I thought that words had a magic and a music quite independent of their meaning." She agreed they did and quoted one of her favorite lines from memory. "His eyes blazed with excitement. 'Say that again,' he said, 'say it again–it is marvelous.'" She quoted still more. "He listened avidly, repeating some lines to himself with varying emphases and stresses." The melody and rhythm of words intoxicated him. Manchester has written that Churchill's feeling "for the English tongue was sensual, almost erotic." When Churchill was chastised for calling Mussolini's actions "at once obsolete and reprehensible," he stood firm. "Ah, the b's in those words: 'obsolete, reprehensible.' You must pay attention to euphony." [163]

This sense of "euphony" fueled his hatred of pompous language and verbosity. He believed that the "jargon of socialism is almost as bad as socialism itself. They do not speak of 'the poor.' No, they say 'marginal stipend maintainers.' They do not talk of 'house' or 'home.' No, it's 'local accommodation unit.' I suppose the Socialists will soon requisition those old samplers our grannies knitted and change them to read 'God bless our local accommodation unit.'" [164] When chastised for ending a sentence with a preposition, he thundered, "This is the sort of English up with which I will not put." He believed that, "Short words are best and the old words when short are best of all." But he could create new words as well. He suggested the word *flight* for a group of planes, devised the word *seaplane*, and urged the term *aeroplane* long before it was in general use.

The impact of this devotion to language upon Churchill's approach to leadership is essential to understanding him. The first step he took in dealing with most any matter was to put it in meaningful terms. He knew that without meaningful words there would be no meaningful understanding and therefore no meaningful action. Stanley Baldwin might say "a bilateral agreement has been reached," but Churchill said simply that they "joined hands together." The Local Defense Volunteers had to be "Home Guard," otherwise who would support it? Once he defined his terms, though, he could move up the abstraction ladder and use the most poetic and moving words to describe his subject, weaving them together in the alternatively thunderous yet sparkling phrasing of his tutors, Gibbon and Macaulay.

Churchill wrote great literature and framed great events for all time because he knew the power and the finesse of his language. He knew that words do more than communicate. They are also the medium of understanding and beauty, the map of the country men seek. The modern world, awash as it is with data parading as knowledge, ought to hear anew Churchill's insistence that words should be used with the precision of the swordsman and the passion of the painter.

THE SPOKEN WORD

"The English language is one of our great sources of inspiration and strength, and no country, or combination, or power so fertile and so vivid exists anywhere else in the world." [165]

Language is one of the great tools of leadership. This is largely because men think and live in terms of the pictures they carry in their hearts, and words craft these pictures. Words are carriers, filled with spirit or meaning or vision, and the images they generate live inside of a man long after he has heard them. When a leader fills his words with truth and vision, he can create on the canvas of the heart the images of a people's destiny and so move them to fulfill it. This is the art of leadership at its best.

Many have heard it said of Winston Churchill that "he mobilized the English language and sent it into battle." Many have also heard the eternal phrases: "finest hour," "broad sunlit uplands," "let us go forward together," "blood, toil, tears and sweat," and "we shall never surrender." And many who remain of an earlier generation remember the comfort and encouragement of his words. Few are aware, however, that Churchill's rhetorical powers did not come naturally for him, but were crafted through tedious effort and hours of practice and study.

Among Churchill's chief obstacles in becoming an effective speaker was his maddening lisp. In his early years he was extremely self-conscious of it. Before going to India, he consulted Sir Felix Semon, a throat specialist, and said, "Cure the impediment in my speech, please. I can't be haunted by the idea that I must avoid every word beginning with an 's.'" Semon told him that there was no organic defect and that "with practice and perseverance" he could be cured. Disappointed but resolute, Churchill devoted himself to "declaiming aloud" whenever in private, and one witness reported seeing him pace up and down a driveway forcing himself to clearly say, "The Spanish ships I cannot see for they are not in sight."

Churchill also wrestled with his inner self in becoming a great speaker. He was very emotional and during his speeches he was often so overcome that tears streamed down his cheeks and he could not continue. It embarrassed him and made some of his speeches uncomfortably sentimental, but he never found the key to containing his emotions. It is good that he did not, since the genius of his words was their passion tempered only by vision and learning, not by stifling self-control.

Churchill also discovered early in his Parliamentary career that he easily got lost in the middle of his thoughts. Since he spoke without notes in the early days, this could result in disaster. Once he was making a speech before the Commons on a trade-union bill and, as usual, he was without notes. He suddenly could not recall a word he intended to say. Utterly undone, he sat down and buried his head in his hands, embarrassed and bewildered.

Nevertheless, it was Churchill's "only ambition to be master of the spoken word," and he was determined to accomplish by effort what he could not through natural ability.[166] He first made peace with his lisp by concluding that an orator can develop a "striking presence" in which a "slight and not unpleasant impediment or stammer" can actually be of assistance in "securing the attention of the audience."[167] He also came to terms with his emotions when he began to see orators as "the embodiment of the passions of the multitude." "Before he can inspire them with any emotion he must be swayed by it himself . . . Before he can move to tears his own must flow."[168] So long as the emotion was not "insincere," it would only abet the speaker's purpose.

The issue then became one of style, and he concluded that "The sentences of the orator when he appeals to his art become long, rolling and sonorous," with "a cadence which resembles blank verse rather than prose."[169] To achieve this, Churchill used several unusual methods. He learned to write his speeches out to the last word and to use a "psalm form" in which each phrase appeared on its own line according to the desired emphasis. This he always did himself, for he never used speech writers. He learned to create the illusion of spontaneity by putting prompts or stage directions in the margins of his text. Cues like "pause: grope for word" and "stammer; correct self" adorned the copy of the speech in his hand, which many in attendance assumed to be notes on issues rather than his full text. To master these, he practiced–sometimes up to eight hours for one speech–in front of a mirror, often doing his best work in the bathtub.

He worked so hard on his speeches that his friends chided him. F. E. Smith said, "Winston has spent the best years of his life writing impromptu speeches." But Churchill knew his limitations: "I am not an orator. An orator is spontaneous."[170]

Instead, he worked on the "carefully prepared impromptu" until it became second nature, and it paid off. "His speeches set the whole kingdom on fire," Lord Ismay said. [171] "He gave you a kind of exaltation. He made you feel that you were taking part in something great and memorable." [172]

But most significant to Churchill would have been the opinion of a Scottish subaltern named Hugh. Dumped with his companions on the roads near Dover after the nightmare of Dunkirk, Hugh was "scared and dazed, and the memory of the Panzers could set us screaming at night." Then, Churchill on the radio: "We shall never surrender." "And I cried when I heard him," Hugh said, "I am not ashamed to say it. And I thought to hell with the Panzers, we're going to win!" [173]

WORK

"I still like work." [174]

One of the gifts of God described in the book of Ecclesiastes is that a man will be able to "rejoice in his labor." [175] How this stands in stark contrast to our own age! Surveys of workers today reveal that most of them hate what they do, would not work if they did not have to, and have little real passion for the activity that consumes at least a third of their lives. Few would place rejoicing in their labors high upon a list of matters about which to beseech the Almighty! There are, though, in this and in every age, those who–without deserving to be called "workaholics"–genuinely love to work, and Winston Churchill was one of them.

Given what he became, it is interesting that more than one of his teachers called him "lazy." Surely this was more for his refusal to dance to the prevailing scholastic tune than for any genuine character flaw. In any case, Winston Churchill evolved into a man with an immense love and capacity for work. The reasons for this transformation bear consideration.

Undoubtedly, part of his motivation came from a determination not to fulfill his father's prophecies. In a fit of anger and disappointment, the declining statesman had written his son, "If you cannot prevent yourself from leading the idle useless unprofitable life you have had during your school days and later months, you will become a mere social wastrel, one of the hundreds of public school failures, and you will degenerate into a shabby unhappy and futile existence." [176] Lord Randolph could hardly have served him better. The specter of failure put fire in Winston's belly and he made it his lifelong mission to outdistance his father's words.

Another source of Winston's capacity for hard work is found in his own self-concept. Often, those who feel less gifted than their peers, who are unable to run on the power of talent and natural ability alone, nevertheless set themselves to the costly hard work their goals demand. This was the case with Churchill. He knew he had talent. But as a late bloomer and as one made to feel insecure and inferior by his teachers and peers, he determined early to accomplish through drive and effort what he thought he could not through ability. No doubt the drive he summoned for such a herculean task was what he sought in the British people during the war years. He knew what it was for the underdog to win through greater passion and harder work.

It is a testimony to his work habits that they even received praise from his detractors. One critic wrote that he was "ill-mannered, boastful, unprincipled, without any redeeming qualities except his amazing ability and industry." [177] His friends, too, lauded his energy. A fellow young politician said that Winston "gave himself to work. When he was not busy with politics, he was reading or writing. He did not lead the life of other young men in London. He may have visited political clubs, but I never met him walking in Pall

Mall or Hyde Park where sooner or later one used to meet one's friends. I never met him at a dinner party that had not some public or some private purpose." [178]

Churchill's appointment book for his first two weeks as an M.P. gives some sense of his industry. During this time he "dined out eight times, attended a trade conference, conducted an inquiry at the Treasury, called on the prime minister, delivered three speeches in the House, campaigned for a Conservative candidate in Manchester, and was there to congratulate him on his victory." [179] Friends were astounded at his output and apparently began to worry about him. The Prince of Wales, the future King Edward VIII, believed he had the solution: "He is so nice, and we have made rather friends. They are worried a little about him, as he has become very spartan–rising at 6 and eating hardly anything. He requires to fall in love with a pretty cat." [180]

Much has been made of Churchill's unusual work habits. To his credit, he found what worked for him and stuck to it. He had witnessed the wonders of the *siesta* in Cuba and began soon after to nap early each afternoon. Far from a sign of laziness, he did this because he discovered that he could gain several additional hours of work late at night when the quiet permitted concentration. Typically, he studied or dictated to a yawning secretary until three in the morning. He then slept late, but as soon as breakfast was served, he again dictated correspondence from a bed strewn with memoranda and official dispatches. Admittedly unorthodox, his schedule permitted incredible efficiency and enabled him to become one of the most productive cabinet members and prime ministers on record.

Beyond productive output, though, Churchill's passionate mastery of hard work developed in him quality and character, which in turn molded his leadership style. He said of one challenge, "The present problem cannot be cured by anything slick, cheap, swift and impatient. It is to be done by hard work in many spheres of action." [181] As a young man on the rise with great ambitions, Winston saw many given to the "slick, cheap, swift and impatient." He saw how little they had to offer and how quickly they passed from the scene. He chose the path of hard work—initially, without doubt, to live down his father's imprecations and to compensate for his own insecurities, but in time as the only route to the greatness he sought. His attitude is best expressed by a verse he cherished throughout his life.

> *The heights of great men reached and kept,*
> *Were not attained by sudden flight,*
> *But they, while their companions slept,*
> *Were toiling upwards in the night.* [182]

Religion

*"I found no comfort in any of the philosophical
ideas which some men parade in their hours of ease
and strength and safety. They seemed only fair-
weather friends. I realized with awful force that no
exercise of my own feeble wit and strength could
save me from my enemies, and that without the
assistance of that High Power which interferes in the
eternal sequence of causes and effects more often
than we are always prone to admit, I could never
succeed. I prayed long and earnestly for help and
guidance. My prayer, as it seems to me, was swiftly
and wonderfully answered."* [183]

There is a schizophrenic nature in modern politics. A
leader is expected to have a religious faith but he is not
supposed to let it influence him in his duties. Somehow, the
truths that determine everything else about his existence are
not allowed to influence how he conducts himself in public
life. Not only that, his principles are usually considered so personal that the public is not even allowed to know for certain

what they are. This passes for noble statecraft in our time. It was once thought cowardice.

Consider, by contrast, the broad stroke, bright color vision of Winston Churchill and the unapologetic manner in which it gushed from his religious faith. In Churchill's world view, there existed an order called "Christian civilization."[184] It was threatened from without by "barbarous paganism"–like Nazism–which spurned "Christian ethics" and derived its "strength and perverted pleasure from persecution."[185] Therefore, every Christian had a "duty to preserve the structure of humane, enlightened, Christian society." This was critical, for "once the downward steps are taken, once one's moral and intellectual feet slipped upon the slope of plausible indulgence, there would be found no halting-place short of a general Paganism and Hedonism." [186]

Convictions such as these elevate temporal struggles to a noble plane and elicit the highest sacrifices. This was the essence of Churchill. He called people to astonishing levels of sacrifice because he summoned them not just to himself or a nation or a philosophy, but to endeavors equal to the eternal realities they already cherished. And this is perhaps the essence of leadership: to connect the temporal to the eternal in search of a more glorious future.

Churchill's own introduction to the eternal was through his nanny, Mrs. Everest. Her influence on him in the early years can hardly be exaggerated, as attested by the picture of her which remained in Winston's bedroom until his death. She was a passionate "low church" believer in the Christian faith. She read Scripture to him, taught him the great hymns, and chiseled prayer into his little heart so skillfully that years later, when in moments of peril, he found himself reciting the prayers he learned at her knee. So strong a symbol of Christianity was she that when a tutor frustrated him in a mathematics lesson, his only recourse with Mrs. Everest was to threaten to "bow down and worship graven images." The lessons ceased…for a season.

The imprint of Mrs. Everest's discipling faded, though, when Winston, as a young Army officer on the Indian frontier, began to read books on religious rationalism. Without a professor or clergyman to guide him, he indiscriminately devoured any available titles on the subject. It shattered his faith. Typical of these years, he wrote his mother, "I do not accept the Christian or any other form of religious beliefs." [187] But this would be short-lived.

While attempting his famous escape from a Boer prison camp during the South African War, he was forced to reconsider his tentative hold on atheism. The idea that his survival depended on his own "wit and strength" drove him to prayer and his escape was so astonishing that he later considered his prayers "wonderfully answered." Indeed, when in desperation he emerged from hiding and identified himself at a township house, he was greeted with a British voice that proclaimed, "Thank God you have come here! It is the only house for twenty miles where you would not have been handed over!" [188] It was easy to see Providence in such good fortune.

Throughout his life, though, his religious faith remained somewhat murky. He liked to quote Disraeli, who said, "Sensible men are all of the same religion." When asked which religion, both men replied, "Sensible men never tell." What is certain is that Churchill despised the vacillations of the institutional church. Of World War I he wrote, "Religion, having discreetly avoided conflict on the fundamental issues, offered its encouragement and consolations through all its forms impartially to all the combatants." [189] Yet, he preached powerful sermons when his role as prime minister demanded it, led Parliament to the Church of St. Margaret, Westminster, to give thanks on V-E Day, and chastised the British Broadcasting Corporation when it gave too much exposure to atheism: "If then, there had been the same devices [televisions] at the time of Christ," he pestered the corporation's decision-makers, "would the BBC give equal time on the air to Judas and Jesus?" [190]

It is interesting to speculate about what might have happened had Churchill entered the church. He apparently considered it. In a letter home from school he once wrote, "Really I feel less keen about the Army every day. I think the Church would suit me better." Years later he pondered, "I might have gone into the Church and preached orthodox sermons in a spirit of audacious contradiction to the age." [191] The fact is, he did preach against the spirit of his age, challenging it with a vision solidly rooted in the Christian world view. Perhaps he thought of himself in the terms he once used to toast his grandson after the child's christening. Turning with pride to the boy he triumphantly proclaimed him "Christ's new faithful soldier and servant." [192]

LOYALTY

"To change your mind is one thing: to turn on those who have followed your previous advice is another."

The measure of a leader is often found in the regard he has for those closest to him. The busier and more powerful a leader becomes, the greater his temptation to stop valuing his intimates as people and to begin dealing with them merely in terms of their contributions to his cause. No longer friends or valued co-laborers, they become hirelings and servants, measured only by their usefulness. When they have been used up and can no longer advance the leader's agenda, he discards them and mentally dissolves them into a sea of indistinguishable faces.

This quality that leaders so quickly lose is simple loyalty. More than blind fealty to useful cronies, it is that genuine and tender faithfulness to a friend or associate that refuses to flee in the face of embarrassment, weakness, or burdensome opposition. Personal loyalty is a critical litmus test of excellence in leadership. If a leader fails to treat those closest to him with warmth and true affection, how can he act with any compassion or humanity in serving a larger and less familiar body? Won't the callousness and cynical abuse he shows to the intimate few simply increase in his dealings with the unfamiliar many?

Winston Churchill certainly had many weaknesses when it came to dealing with people. He was often arrogant, always impatient, and unquestionably self-centered. But he was also loyal, intensely so, particularly to his friends. Friendship meant a great deal to Churchill. He often experienced loneliness even when he wasn't alone and the few real friends he had, those who stayed with him in the darkest hours, were more precious to him than life. Brendan Bracken, one of his dearest companions, said: "He would go to the stake for a friend." [193] His friends were small in number; but he loved and honored them, and they knew it.

An early hint of Churchill's immense capacity for loyalty is glimpsed in his relationship with Mrs. Everest, his nanny from infancy. His affection for her was unbridled, as it was she who "looked after me and tended all my wants. It was to her I poured out my many troubles." [194] He told his parents that more than anything else, he associated her with "home" since she was more devoted to him than "any other people in the world." [195] The incident that demonstrated his courageous loyalty to her occurred when she visited him at Harrow. Though little boys were usually quite ashamed of their nannies then, Winston defied the trend. He "paraded his old nurse, immensely fat and all smiles, down High Street, and then unashamedly kissed her in full view of his schoolmates." A witness called the kiss "one of the bravest acts I have ever seen." [196] Winston, deeply proud of his beloved nanny, could not have cared less about the opinions of his chums. His steadfast loyalty was such that when the old woman died he was there, tenderly holding her hand. When Churchill died, seventy years later, her picture was at his side.

The more famous expression of Churchill's passionate sense of loyalty was when he publicly supported his friend, King Edward VIII, in what came to be known as "the abdication crisis." Edward was the King of England and as such, the "Defender of the Faith"–a Church of England faith that did not recognize divorce. When Edward fell in love with Mrs. Wallis Simpson, an American divorcee, and expressed intentions to marry her, it meant nothing less than his stepping down from the throne.

Churchill was one of the few who supported his sovereign and it cost him dearly. His wife, the prime minister, and his closest friends bitterly disagreed with him, but Churchill said, "I should have been ashamed if, in my independent and unofficial position, I had not cast about for any lawful means, even the most forlorn, to keep him on the Throne of his fathers." [197] A friend wrote that Churchill "would have been prepared to stand alone beside his King against a world of arms." [198] He virtually did. When he rose in Parliament to defend Edward, he suffered what an observer called "one of the angriest manifestations I have ever heard directed against any man in the House of Commons." [199] The roar of opposition was deafening and when the Speaker ruled him out of order, Churchill stormed out, screaming at Prime Minister Baldwin, "You won't be satisfied until you've broken him, will you?" Later, when the King abdicated, the always loyal Churchill not only wept openly but wrote the speech Edward delivered to the nation explaining his actions.

Churchill's sense of loyalty contained an amazing amount of tolerance. His secretary, Eddie Marsh, was reputed to be a homosexual, but Churchill refused to entertain the slightest accusation about the matter, even those from his own mother. Similarly, as vehemently as he objected to Prime Minister Chamberlain's policies, Churchill rebuffed repeated attacks by Harold Macmillan calling for Chamberlain's ouster. "I have signed on for the voyage," he proclaimed, "and would stick to the ship."[200] He was not always so gracious, however. When those to whom he felt loyalty were attacked, it often sent him into a rage. On one occasion, his son Randolph was humiliated from the floor of Parliament by a Conservative back bencher. When Churchill confronted the opponent in the corridor, he screamed, "Do not speak to me. You called my son a coward. You are my enemy. Do not speak to me."[201] It was the raw, unthinking loyalty of a father.

Churchill's life was powered by an unswerving allegiance to his principles, his nation, and his dearest friends. But in his unquestioning commitment to others, in his almost romantic fidelity to those who stood with him, one sees at work the passion that lifted his gifts for leadership to an exceptional level. Undoubtedly, this is the root of his greatness: the common raised to inspiring and commanding heights by uncommon loyalty to something beyond self.

HERITAGE

"Fortune is rightly malignant to those who break with the customs of the past." [202]

One of the signs of a great society is the diligence with which it passes culture from one generation to the next. This culture is the embodiment of everything the people of that society hold dear: its religious faith, its heroes, and its traditions, arts, and ceremonies. When one generation no longer esteems its own heritage and fails to pass the torch to its children, it is saying in essence that the very foundational principles and experiences that make the society what it is are no longer valid. This, of course, leaves that next generation without any sense of definition or direction, making them the fulfillment of Karl Marx's dictum, "A people without a heritage are easily persuaded."

What is required when this happens and the society has lost its way is for leaders to arise who have not forgotten the discarded legacy and who love it with all their hearts. They can then become the voice of that lost heritage, wooing an errant generation back to the faith of the fathers, back to the ancient foundations and the bedrock values and traditions. In England, during the first half of the twentieth century, the voice and embodiment of heritage was Winston Churchill, who loved Christendom, empire, monarchy, and his "island race" as much as any man could. Before it was too late, before a heritage of centuries was discarded by neglect or conquest, Churchill cried out for his nation to remember and reclaim.

As a historian, Churchill studied societies that disconnected themselves from their historical moorings. He discovered that when a generation isolates itself from its past and begins to measure progress only in terms of its own accumulations, the history of that civilization begins drawing to a close. Churchill concluded that what holds society together from generation to generation are those shared values and traditions that comprise heritage. Civilizations can only thrive from age to age when the legacy each generation receives from its ancestors is passed on in strengthened form to their children.

It is not putting it too strongly to say that Churchill saw as his life's purpose the reviving of the glory of Christendom and the strengthening of the British empire as Christendom's stronghold. On June 18, 1940, Churchill spoke in the House of Commons about the implications of France, under the leadership of Marshal Petain, having sued for peace with Nazi Germany. "I expect that the Battle of Britain is about to begin," he thundered. "Upon this battle depends the survival of Christian civilization. Upon it depends our own British life, and the long continuity of our institutions and our Empire." [203] Here is the twin force of the Churchill juggernaut: Christian civilization and British heritage. In an age still smarting from the horrors of World War I–an age when patriotism and love of country were suspect–Churchill unashamedly proclaimed himself an advocate of Christian England: "At all times, according to my lights and throughout the changing scenes through which we are all hurried, I have always faithfully served two public causes which, I think, stand supreme–the maintenance of the enduring greatness of Britain and her Empire, and the historical continuity of our island life." [204]

These attitudes were woven into the fabric of Churchill's personality and world view. He once said, "I confess myself to be a great admirer of tradition," and those who knew him were astonished by how rooted in tradition and heritage he really was. [205] Clement Attlee once compared Churchill to a layer cake: "One layer was certainly seventeenth century. The eighteenth century in him is obvious. There was the nineteenth century, and a large slice of course, of the twentieth century; and another, curious, layer which may possibly have been the twenty-first." [206] The genius of Churchill is that he was not stuck in any one of these layers but that he sought to build upon each of them. He would have argued that strong civilizations are also like a layer cake and when any one layer is ignored or removed, it weakens the whole.

This was Churchill's fear about his own age. Through the course of his long life, he had watched the gradual erosion of vital Christianity as a cultural force in England. He grieved at the loss of honor, respect, and humility that resulted. But what really alarmed him were the many new untested philosophies that rushed in to claim the seat of power Christianity once had held. Each of these new schemes fell disastrously short of the traditional values and the Christian culture they sought to replace. "Those who seek to plan the future," Churchill warned, "should not forget the inheritance they have received from the past, for it is only by studying the past as well as drawing for the future that the story of man's struggle can be understood." [207]

Remembering that Churchill lived not only through the Victorian era, but also through the cataclysms of two world wars, not to mention the revolutionary decades of the 1950's and the 1960's, it is not hard to understand how difficult it must have been for him to witness the decline of the Christian order in which he was born and which he loved so dearly. No wonder he believed that "If the present tries to sit in judgment of the past, it will lose the future."[208] He saw twentieth century man sitting in judgment on the past only to find it wanting and it worried him for the future of mankind.

Nevertheless, he believed there was hope. In a revealing meeting with evangelist Billy Graham in 1954, Churchill discussed the condition of the world and how vastly different it was from the time of his youth. He then told Graham, "I do not see much hope for the future unless it is the hope you are talking about, young man. We must have a return to God."[209] Clearly, Churchill hoped that his generation would recover what it had not accepted from the generations before it: faith in God and the culture that faith produces. It was, he believed, the hope of mankind, "of Christian civilization" and the "continuity of our institutions and our Empire."

THE WILDERNESS

*"Every prophet has to come from civilization, but
every prophet has to go into the wilderness. He must
have a strong impression of a complex society and
all that it has to give, and then he must serve periods of isolation and meditation. This is the process
by which psychic dynamite is made."* [210]

There is a force in modern life that some have called the
"herd mentality." It grows from the idea, drilled so effectively into the minds of youth today, that the group must be
right simply because it is the group. The promise is com-
pelling: peace and security are found only within the fortress
of the many and so men ought to live their lives wisely guided
by the expectations of the majority. Deviation is sickness; non-
conformity the vilest sin. Such is the faith of a people who
have lost their moorings in the eternal. It is the religion of our
times, the religion of the people: *vox populi, vox dei*–the voice
of the people is the voice of God.

But then who shall lead the people? Those who are prod-
ucts of society have no creative alternatives to offer. The system

produces nothing that challenges the system. The surge of the masses cannot produce leaders: demagogues and media icons–yes, but not leaders. Leaders are rare. Leaders, like diamonds, are shaped by unrelenting opposition at work on the best of raw materials. The true leader has something to offer only because he has stood apart from his civilization long enough to view it as though for the first time. Indeed, what so often distinguishes the truly great leader is his willingness to pay the price of his vision in the coin of rejection and isolation. Then, no longer swept along by the currents of his age, he is able to rise above it and lead.

Winston Churchill was a great leader. He exercised power at a time when the clash of titanic forces made his every move of global importance. His words were household sayings, his image a familiar and comforting sight to millions. Even today, it is not hard to remember the bulldog demeanor, the jaunty cigar, and two-fingered sign of victory. Churchill made himself the very symbol of resistance and then later the embodiment of victory. He is today no less than the metaphor of greatness and leadership. Yet, those who honor Churchill rarely consider the price he paid for his role in history. His "psychic dynamite," which so commanded the world stage in the years of crises, was fashioned during lonely years of heartrending ridicule and isolation.

It began during his earliest experiences in school. Through his parents' neglect he was abandoned to a public school world largely devoid of love or intimacy. During these years, he suffered not only the aching loneliness of his isolation from family and friends, but also the rejection that comes from being different. He was smaller than the other boys in his school and did not perform well in the classroom or on the playing field. This made him a special target of the fagging and hazing common in those days. And he drew more than his share of abuse because he was cocky, brash, and often insolent. He would be, he assured his mates, "a great man" one day, and they ought to know it. Such prophecies met with unceasing abuse and condemnation. Soon he acquired the mentality of the outsider, forever wrestling with a combination of self-doubt and distrust of those around him.

Neither feats of glory in service of the Queen's empire nor literary and political successes could make him an insider at heart. On the eve of his wedding, which came uncommonly late in life, he wrote his wife-to-be, "I am a solitary creature in the midst of crowds. Be kind to me." [211] She was, and her love and healing care often sustained him in the shattering seasons of rejection that marked his career. Time and again the reins of power, for which he knew he was destined, were torn from his hands as he was driven into agonizing political and social isolation. It happened following the Dardanelles disaster of World War I. It happened again when the Baldwin/MacDonald coalition excluded him in 1929, marking for him the beginning of a wilderness decade that ended only with the onset of World War II. And it happened when the British people, in an astounding move, voted him out of office after their victory—indeed, his victory–over Nazi Germany.

Churchill was not immune to the tortures of these dark periods. Yet, it is not hard to see how his approach to them did much to make him the leader he was. When faith that he would one day return to power combined with the fresh perspective afforded by his isolation, he saw the future–and began to prepare for it. He learned to farm the valleys of his life, and later found the fruit of his labors sweet and sustaining against the press of battle.

In the wilderness years he drew strength from his family, faced down his "Black Dog" depressions, and peered intently into the matters of his soul and destiny. He studied the world scene, assembled a valued team of advisors, wrote great works of insightful history, and attempted to rouse an endangered but deceived nation with stirring words. True, his lone voice from the wilderness was the subject of cruel jokes in the fashionable parlors of England, but Churchill was right and he knew it. He knew it because he was not in those fashionable parlors, but standing in the harsh yet clarifying light of abandonment, ridicule, and seclusion. It is the price the prophet pays. Only one who has paid this price can say to his people, as Churchill did to England in the war years, "We shall draw from the heart of suffering itself the means of inspiration and survival." [212]

Future

"I have no fear of the future. Let us go forward into its mysteries, let us tear aside the veils which hide it from our eyes and let us move onward with confidence and courage." [213]

*L*eadership has a great deal to do with the future. This is largely because men live out, in practical terms, what they believe about the future. When prophets of doom paint a dark and foreboding picture of the days to come, men almost automatically begin to live in terms of the narrow and the short term. They shrink in fear from risk, become compulsively self-centered, and insulate themselves with the instant and the sensual. On the other hand, when men see their future as one of promise and fruitfulness, they start living boldly and expansively, they take the risks necessary for success, and they start thinking in terms of generations yet unborn. Throughout history great leaders have demonstrated that the ability to project a gripping vision of the future is at the very heart of exceptional leadership.

Winston Churchill's passionate vision of the future was among the most potent of the weapons in his arsenal. Just as he believed in his own personal destiny, he also had faith in what he called "the mission of mankind."[214] He believed that history as a whole and all the ages in it are being drawn to a glorious conclusion by the same God who created the universe. He trusted that mankind is destined for good, that progress is inevitable, and that every age should contribute to the upward climb of civilization. Since, in Churchill's philosophy, the future gives meaning to the present, the mightiest men in any generation would be those with the clearest vision of what is to come. Churchill determined to be among them.

This intense interest in the future arose from several sources. Its seeds are in the heart of the small, neglected boy, alone in his private boarding school, anxiously awaiting the next respite from his agonizing isolation. For year after torturous year, what lay ahead for him was all that made what he was living through bearable. The jaunty optimism of his age also contributed to his hopeful view of history. He was unquestionably influenced by the romance and power of Queen Victoria's empire and he eagerly participated in the natural confidence of a nation that ruled one quarter of the world and anticipated no end to its dominion. Also of great impact was his adherence to the historiography of the Enlightenment. That reasonable men applying natural law could build enduring utopias was a bright expectation of eighteenth-century Europe. Churchill shared its hope.

In the early 1940's, a poster of an intent, finger-pointing Churchill was plastered all over England. The bold words accompanying Churchill's image summoned the best the nation had to offer. They read simply, "Deserve Victory!" It was Churchill's life philosophy. "What is the use of living," he asked, "if it be not to strive for noble causes and to make this muddled world a better place to live in after we are gone?"[215] The future was his compass, and when he called others to live by it, they were changed. It was as though he was saying, "Think what your actions now will mean, years hence, when you remember them again. What kind of person will you wish you had been, what kind of sacrifices will you wish you had made, when you or those who survive you look back upon this from the future?" With this perspective at heart, men rose above themselves.

He taught his people to see themselves in terms of what others would say "if the British Empire and its Commonwealth last for a thousand years."[216] They should be comforted in battle by the day "when history is written and all the facts are known,"[217] and fight to "win that world [the future] for our children."[218] Failure meant sinking "into the abyss of a new Dark Age made more sinister, and perhaps more protracted, by the lights of perverted science."[219] Victory meant "the survival of Christian civilization" and the "continuity of our institutions and our Empire."[220] It meant men would "come through these dark and dangerous valleys into a sunlight broader and more genial and more lasting than mankind has ever known."[221] These were the "broad sunlit uplands" Churchill promised.

To know the future more fully, he studied the past. "Learn all you can about the history of the past," he wrote, "for how else can one even make a guess what is going to happen in the future?"[222] After all, "The farther backward you can look, the farther forward you can see."[223] His studies enabled him to see much further than most men and his predictions of future events were astounding. He spoke of the eight-hour workday in 1901, the importance of air power for the next world war in 1917, the atomic bomb in 1917, and the energy crisis in 1928. Though experts mocked him, he was ahead of his time in warning the world of the Nazis, the Iron Curtain, and the bog of Vietnam. The future was familiar country to him.

Nevertheless, he had great respect for the uncertainties of time. "It is not given to us to peer into the mysteries of the future," he said. "It is a mistake to look too far ahead. Only one link in the chain of destiny can be handled at a time." [224] Even in this humility, though, it was exactly his belief in a "chain of destiny"–in a connection of ages culminating in a brilliant future–that gave Churchill such captivating vision. He painted what he saw of the future in the faith-inspiring words others called the language of leadership. For Churchill, though, it was the excitement of a man who has discovered an important truth about life–and of moving men to their best.

Death

"When the notes of life ring false, men should correct them by referring to the tuning fork of death." [225]

Visitors to the great cathedrals of Europe are usually astonished to discover that the walls and columns of these awe-inspiring temples are routinely adorned with replicas of human skulls. "They are there," explained one elderly cathedral steward, "so that men might contemplate their mortality." Clearly, the generations of Christians who built these great houses of worship did not consider death an unpleasant topic to be avoided, but rather a vantage point from which to gain perspective on life. They looked death in the face, seized its reality, and made it their servant. "Death is the destiny of every man," they would have said with the writer of Ecclesiastes, "the living should take this to heart." [226]

Winston Churchill took this admonition very much to heart. Throughout his life, he attempted to learn what death had to teach. He tried to think of his life and his contribution to mankind as though from the grave, as though his days were done and the measure of his existence was in terms of the eternal. When all the clatter of this world had passed, what would be the real meaning of his life? How much good would he really have accomplished, measured in terms of a year or two years or decades beyond the grave? By looking on his days in this way, Churchill allowed death to be the tuning fork for his life, the one consistent pitch by which he could measure the truthfulness of all the others.

Death became a very personal force for Churchill early in his life. Not only did he come close to the end many times due to his frequent and severe childhood illnesses, but in one particular near-fatal incident he saw the face of death so clearly that he never forgot its visage. The incident occurred during a walking tour in Switzerland when Churchill was a teenager. He and his brother Jack went rowing on the lake of Lausanne and once they had gone a good distance, they decided to throw off their clothes and enjoy a swim. As they swam, the wind began to gently move the boat away from them. They finally noticed when the boat was nearly a thousand yards away and though they tried desperately to catch it, the harder they swam toward the boat, the further the wind seemed to push it away.

At that moment the specter of death appeared before young Winston. "I now saw death as near as I believe I have ever seen Him. He was swimming in the water at our side, whispering from time to time in the rising wind which continued to carry the boat away from us at about the same speed we could swim." Churchill eventually reached the boat and rowed back for Jack, whom, he was convinced, "had not realized the dull yellow glare of mortal peril that had so suddenly played around us." [227] The memory of this near-tragedy stayed with Churchill throughout his life.

This is not to say that he had a morbid preoccupation with death. It is true that he was often plagued by thoughts of suicide during his "Black Dog" depressions. It is also true that he endured the deaths of many who were close to him, whether comrades on the battlefield, lifelong friends whom he simply outlived, or even two of his own dear daughters. Yet none of these experiences kept him from nurturing a healthy lightheartedness. "I am ready to meet my Maker," he said in a speech on his birthday in 1951. "Whether my maker is prepared for the great ordeal of meeting me is another matter." [228] And in a typically Churchillian tease: "We make too much of it. All religions do. Of course, I may alter my views." [229]

Churchill could joke about his death, though, because he did not fear it. He knew not only that it was inevitable, but also that it was a glorious liberation into the next life. "Noble spirits," he wrote in his biography of Marlborough, "yield themselves willingly to the successively falling shades which carry them to a better world or to oblivion." This same view was reflected in one of the most beautiful of his speeches, the one he gave upon the death of his friend, King George VI.

> *He was sustained not only by his natural buoyancy but by the sincerity of his Christian faith. During these last months the King walked with death as if death were a companion, an acquaintance whom he recognized and did not fear. In the end death came as a friend, and, after a happy day of sunshine and sport, and after "Good night" to those who loved him best, he fell asleep as every man or woman who strives to fear God and nothing else in the world may hope to do.* [230]

For men who lack faith, death is to be feared above all things. For men who have faith, death has lost its sting.

Churchill knew this, and knew that keeping death in view gave him the ability to measure the genuineness and the importance of the things he pursued in life. It kept him humble, mindful that real life had not yet begun. By living in the present in terms of the eternal, he achieved a greatness that death cannot destroy.

WINSTON CHURCHILL: THE LEGACY OF LEADERSHIP

ᴑᴑ   ᴑᴑ   ᴑᴑ

"One mark of a great man is the power of making lasting impressions upon the people he meets."

"When the eagles are silent, the parrots begin to jabber."

"THE LONG SHADOW"

The issue of Winston Churchill's place in history may have been decided once and for all in the weeks just before his ninetieth birthday. Among the many other cards and greetings that arrived for him, there was one that particularly stood out. It had been crafted by a nine-year-old girl and mailed without a stamp from Colombia, South America. Yet it arrived at 28 Hyde Park Gate, Churchill's London residence, because of the unusual way it was addressed: the envelope read only "To the Greatest Man in the World."

Churchill was indeed a great man and certainly among the greatest in history. He is perhaps the most revered, quoted, discussed, and emulated leader of modern times. Yet, what confirms Churchill's overshadowing place in history is not just what he accomplished during his own lifetime, but also the relevance of his enduring legacy. In an age when leaders pass from the scene rapidly and without much loss, Churchill remains astoundingly relevant and contemporary. One suspects it will remain so for generations. The reason is that Churchill was, stating it plainly, a wise man; not a wise man in the sense of the eastern mystic, but rather of a man who has lived deeply, whose wisdom was born in study, tempered in conflict, tested in crisis, and honed in reflection. It was a wisdom beyond his own age, a kind that transcended his times and has relevance for every age in which men grapple with mighty causes. Consider, for example, these words in light of the recent crises in the former Yugoslavia.

> *If Europe is to be saved from infinite misery, and indeed from final doom, there must be an act of faith in the European family and an act of oblivion against all the crimes and follies of the past. Then, the wrongs and injuries which have been inflicted will have been washed away on all sides by the miseries which have been endured. Is there any need for further floods of agony? Is it the only lesson of history that mankind is unteachable? Let there be justice, mercy and freedom. The peoples have only to will it, and all will achieve their hearts desire.*[1]

Even a cursory glance through the most recent books on world affairs show how important Churchill is. In his last book, *Beyond Peace*, Richard Nixon quoted Churchill twice and together the well-known expressions virtually summarize the whole of Nixon's thesis: First, "Russia fears our friendship more than our enmity."[2] Second, "Democracy is the worst form of government except for all the others."[3] Likewise, in their international best seller, *The Great Reckoning*, James Davidson and Lord Rees Mogg can do no better in describing the decline of America than to quote Churchill's lament for Great Britain: "I have watched this famous island descending incontinently, fecklessly, the stairway which leads to a dark gulf. It is a fine broad stairway at the beginning, but after a bit the carpet ends. A little farther on there are only flagstones, and little farther on still these break beneath your feet."[4] And who can fault the authors for relying on such powerful expressions as, "Many itching fingers were stretching and scratching at the vast pillage of a derelict empire."[5]

On an astounding range of issues, Churchill's views approach prophecy. He anticipated that technology would raise enormous questions of morality and privacy. He expected the ruin of Christendom, the increase of statism, and a tragic loss of individual liberties. Indeed, most of the matters Churchill devoted his life to are issues in our own time: the European Common Market, Romania, Bosnia, Poland, the Middle East, and Russia. Even Churchill's thoughts about an event like D-Day anticipated much of modern scholarship. In a letter to General Eisenhower, Churchill wrote, "Historians will consider and describe it as a great military movement, but I must tell you, my dear general, it was the fourth-best possibility."[6] Many now see it as Churchill did so long ago.

It is no surprise then that leaders of every political persuasion invoke the name of Churchill. They use his quotes, his politics, and even his humor in hopes of approaching his greatness. But in spite of their best efforts, they fail. John Naisbitt, in his ground-breaking study of world trends, *Global Paradox*, has written that men today are crying aloud, "Where are the Churchills?"[7] It is a cry for leadership, for strength and resolve, but the more men strive to emulate what they think made Churchill great, the wider the gap between themselves and the "Great Man" grows. This is because when they study Churchill to glean "leadership insights," they come away with what amounts to a bag of tricks. They use him to hone the craft of making themselves appear what they are not.

What they miss, though, and what even Churchill's peers missed about him, is that Churchill's greatness was not first and foremost a matter of externals. His greatness was and still remains a matter of the heart–of faith and values and religion–and when modern secularists attempt to imitate Churchill without taking on the very faith and Christian world view that shaped his life and leadership, they engage in meaningless theatrics. Churchill was a Christian who saw the world in Christian terms and this was the power behind everything he was as a man of global consequence.

THE FAITH OF CHURCHILL

*U*nfortunately, historians have been largely unwilling to recognize the influence of Christianity in Churchill's life. This is for several reasons, the most important of which is that modern historians rarely deal seriously with Christianity at all, much less with its impact on the lives of famous individuals. In the halls of academe, it is assumed that we live today in a post-Christian age, that the Christian gospel is the true source of evil behind the historic abuse of minorities, the environment and the human psyche, and that any adherence to Christian principles on the part of political leaders is pure window dressing. The resulting revisionism gives us American history textbooks that never mention the faith of men like Columbus, Washington and Lincoln, or that confidently assert that the Pilgrim fathers held the first Thanksgiving feast to give thanks to the Indians.

A second reason for the refusal to deal with Churchill's faith is that his times did not require him to go out of his way to establish himself publicly as a believer and this has left very little of the kind of "hard" evidence historians prefer. Churchill was, after all, a devoted son of the Anglican church during the great Victorian age in British history. It was assumed that England was a Christian nation, that her leaders were committed to the Gospel of Christ, and that Christian morality was the universal standard of decency. In such an age Churchill's faith could well be genuine and deep without being particularly notable. He was not, remember, a cleric or, like C. S. Lewis, a Christian apologist. He was a man who assumed the truth of Christianity and acted accordingly in the political arena. Yet, in the absence of abundant hard evidence for Churchill's Christian faith, historians have largely chosen to ignore what evidence there is and to present Churchill as a confirmed non-believer.

Examples of this approach abound. The two weightiest Churchill scholars, Martin Gilbert and William Manchester, deal with issues like Churchill's attitude toward the Jews and the sexual antics of his mother in far greater detail than they do the issue of his religious faith. Others historians have taken a more strident stance. Piers Brendon, in his *Winston Churchill: A Biography*, concluded that Churchill "had no real belief in the Christian dispensation, no faith in God, no hope of heaven." [8] John Pearson, who has written about Churchill in *The Private Lives of Winston Churchill*, apparently had similar doubts. Pearson described Churchill's funeral as "a great religious celebration for this stalwart non-believer" and complained that at the death bed "there was even a priest to give the blessing of a God in whom he never had believed." [9]

Since studies such as these have helped to create the popular myth of Churchill as an unshakable atheist, it must have caught more than one listener by surprise when Billy Graham, speaking at the funeral of Richard Nixon, drew back the veil on a Winston Churchill few had ever seen.

Years ago, Winston Churchill planned his own funeral, and he did so with the hope of the resurrection and eternal life, which he firmly believed in. And he instructed after the benediction that a bugler positioned high in the dome of Saint Paul's Cathedral would play "Taps"– the universal signal that says the day is over. But then came a very dramatic moment as Churchill had instructed. Another bugler was placed on the other side of the massive dome, and he played the notes of "Reveille"–the universal signal that a new day has dawned and it is time to arise. That was Churchill's testimony–that at the end of history the last note will not be "Taps." It will be "Reveille." [10]

How unusual this must have seemed to a people familiar with only the image of Churchill as a drunken, cigar-chomping pagan. The Churchill that Billy Graham described was a man who believed in eternal life and the promise of the resurrection. This Churchill was not only a believer, but a man who went out of his way to proclaim his faith by dramatically symbolizing it in his own funeral.

Yet this "resurrected" Churchill ought not have been that surprising. Churchill never hid his faith, but he also never paraded it for political advantage and perhaps here is where the confusion lies. Perhaps the modern world is so used to carnal public figures who talk loudly about their religious lives that it is mystified by a man who quietly applied the assumptions of a Biblical world view to his work and spoke unashamedly of his faith when the need arose, but never felt obligated to crassly advertise himself as a believer. Perhaps the tension here is actually between modern politicians who *look* like Christians but *act* like pagans and a man like Churchill who usually sported a cigar (though it was unlit most of the time), who enjoyed liquor as one of his cultured pleasures (though he actually drank very little), but who faithfully built his life in public service upon the distinctives of a Christian world view.

If there is confusion about Churchill's faith, though, it is not because he was unclear about what he believed. He explained that he was first influenced in matters of faith and politics by his father, Lord Randolph, "the man with that strong religious strain in his nature."[11] He also admitted that he was deeply affected by the simple strength of Mrs. Everest's faith, that he underwent a troubling anti-religious phase when he immersed himself in rationalistic theology on the Indian frontier, and that he recovered himself when he later found his prayers marvelously answered in times of danger. What is more, he was emphatic about his faith in Scripture, his commitment to the miraculous, and his confidence in a divine destiny. He went so far as to say that he preferred Protestantism over Catholicism because "the Reformed Church is less deeply sunk in the mire of dogma than the Oriental Establishment."

He even defended orthodox Christianity against the onslaught of rationalism and theological liberalism. In an article entitled simply, *Moses,* Churchill took an opposing stance to the forces that were so disastrously undercutting Biblical faith in his day and, in doing so, he established his own orthodox view of Scripture.

> *We reject, however, with scorn all those learned and laboured myths that Moses was but a legendary figure upon whom the priesthood and the people hung their essential social, moral and religious ordinances. We believe that the*

> *most scientific view, the most up-to-date and*
> *rationalistic conception, will find its fullest sat-*
> *isfaction in taking the Bible story literally, and*
> *in identifying one of the greatest of human*
> *beings with the most decisive leap-forward ever*
> *discernible in the human story.*[12]

In that same article, Churchill confirmed his faith not only in the God of the Bible, but also in His government over the affairs of men.

> *All these purely rationalistic and scientific*
> *explanations only prove the truth of the Bible*
> *story. It is silly to waste time arguing whether*
> *Jehovah broke His own natural laws to save*
> *His Chosen People or whether He merely made*
> *them work in a favourable manner. At any rate*
> *there is no doubt about one miracle. This wan-*
> *dering tribe, in many respects indistinguishable*
> *from numberless nomadic communities,*
> *grasped and proclaimed an idea of which all*
> *the genius of Greece and all the power of Rome*
> *were incapable. There was to be only one God,*
> *a universal God, a God of nations, a just God, a*
> *God who would punish in another world a*
> *wicked man dying rich and prosperous, a God*
> *from whose service the good of the humble and*
> *of the weak and the poor was inseparable.*[13]

This high view of divine providence, coupled with a profoundly spiritual understanding of history, led Churchill into passionate devotion to that earthly expression of the kingdom of Christ called Christendom. He firmly believed that

Christianity was the wellspring of Western culture and that "On that system and by that faith there has been built out of the wreck of the Roman Empire the whole of our existing civilisation."[14] In support of a 1901 Ecclesiastical Law, Churchill wrote:

> ...this [law], in itself important, was only a single instance of our duty to preserve the structure of humane, enlightened, Christian society. Once the downward steps were taken, once one's moral and intellectual feet slipped upon the slope of plausible indulgence, there would be found no halting-place short of a general Paganism and Hedonism, possibly agreeable from time to time in this world of fleeting trials and choices, but fatal hereafter through measureless ages, if not indeed through eternity itself.[15]

For Churchill, history was a stage for the great unfolding drama of Christian civilization. He wanted to be an actor in that drama, a commander of Christian armies marching for the victory of Christendom, and this explains how Christianity shaped Churchill's perception of his role in public affairs.

How, then, can Churchill's place in history be determined apart from his faith and the Christian character it produced? Churchill's life must be seen the way he saw it: in terms of a distinctly Christian heritage and world view. Unless one understands Churchill's almost romantic attachment to the fading glory of Christendom, unless one hears the lion's roar of Christian England, and unless one accepts that a twentieth century politician might quietly see himself as a misplaced medieval knight in the service of Christ, one can never hope to comprehend the reason for Churchill's greatness.

Yet, this raises an important question: Why haven't Christians paid more attention to the life and faith of Winston Churchill? One suspects that it is partially because Churchill, though a committed believer, was not an exceptionally pious man. Beyond this, though, is the reality that Christian histories tend to focus on preachers and those who are "in the ministry" as it is traditionally defined. This overlooks, however, the whole range of Christian activity that is not "the ministry" but rather the application of the Gospel to the marketplace of human activity. What of the believers whose "ministry" is to be a redemptive force in business, the arts, or politics? What of the men and women who are called to follow in the footsteps of a William Wilberforce, the British Parliamentarian who led the move to outlaw slavery in Victorian England, or a Rembrandt van Rijn, or the host of Christian businessmen and financiers who have funded the work of "the ministry" throughout the world. Perhaps when Christians again appreciate the Reformation doctrine that vocation is calling and that most of the truly dramatic confrontations between darkness and light take place in the marketplace and not in the pulpits of churches, Churchill's life will be treated by Christians with the interest and reverence it deserves.

This is all the more important because the real issue in leadership, again, is character. Genuine faith produces character, and proven character is the basis of all true greatness. In Churchill's life, those Christian virtues that he labored so manfully to perfect are what laid the foundation for his success. His physical and moral courage, his endurance in the face of crushing difficulty, and his ability to see the world not as it was but as faith could make it–all this was the product of a character borne of faith. This is what set Churchill apart, what he symbolized, projected, and implanted in others. And this is what brought letters to his hand addressed only "To the Greatest Man in the World."

THE PILLARS OF GREATNESS

*F*or those, then, who wish to go the way of Churchill, who seek to contend with perhaps lesser foes than he but with like courage and force, what are the essential elements of his unique style of life and leadership?

First, Churchill was a believer. This is not to say that he was a man of deep personal piety or spiritual discipline, but rather that he was completely accepting of the claims of Scripture and the teachings of historic Christianity. Yet, beyond this, Churchill's legacy of faith is that he conducted himself in events of global importance within the framework of a biblical world view. He was the kind of man who would not believe something he could not act on, but when he accepted the distinctives of a Christian understanding of the world, it was not long before his actions, policies, and hopes began to reflect his undergirding faith. This is far preferable to the kind of leader who believes much but does little. Churchill believed carefully, but he believed passionately, and accordingly the fate of nations was entrusted into his hands.

Second, Churchill was truly a man. In fact, if there is anything true of Winston Churchill it is that he was given to the fullest expression of what it means to be a man. In an age when leaders typically looked and acted like they spent their spare time parsing Greek verbs, Churchill commanded respect because he roared into life with a muscular, wholly masculine energy. Soldiers in the trenches knew that their prime minister had stood in similar battle lines and choked back the same fear that gnawed at their insides. Churchill knew what it was to kill, to suffer hunger and thirst, to live only for the moment, and to have friends who meant more than life itself. He knew the raw and the violent and the horrible. But he was also a man of culture, music, painting, literature, and thought. And all this diverse experience was recorded in a heart at once proud yet searching, at once fierce yet compassionate–as the hearts of men tend to be. Winston Churchill was a man, and his willingness to embrace everything that that means made him a leader of exceptional complexity and power.

Third, Churchill was a dreamer. People who intend to create change must have the ability to see beyond what is to what can be. They must be able to dream without making dreams their master. Churchill was this kind of dreamer. When he bought Chartwell, for example, he bought only the raw material of a dream. It was his job to impose his dream on the land by building, moving, digging, sculpting, and growing the land into its glory. So it was with his painting. Churchill studied landscapes but painted improvements. If the colors of nature were not brilliant enough, he simply added them. It was the same with mountain ranges, rivers, lakes, and forests: if they weren't in reality, they were in the dream and should be painted. This is exactly how Churchill led nations to victory. First, victory had to be in the dream, had to be visualized beyond reality. But then, once the vision was identified, it was simply a matter of conforming reality to the dream through faith and hard work. Leaders have to be dreamers because they must be able to "see" the promised land in order to enter it.

Fourth, Churchill was a thinker. Leaders have to walk a fine line between thought and action. If they settle into thought for too long, they tend to slip into an ethereal lethargy. If they move through thought too rapidly in pursuit of action, they tend to act unwisely and destructively. The best combination is a thinking process that reduces the issues to simple terms so that meaningful, informed action can ensue. This means that leaders should be philosophers, as Churchill was, but only in the looser sense. That is,

> *in which a man who has touched life at many points may comment at large upon men and things, distilling in aphorisms and epigrams, in maxims and exhortations, the ripe fruits of his mellow experience. The philosopher so conceived is akin to the sage or wise man of the East; experience has ripened in him a faculty of insight which enables him to see farther into things than his fellows, and to embody what he has seen in pregnant observations.*[16]

The purpose of the leader's voyage into this looser philosophy is to distill the principles and maxims that permit action. This is what distinguished Churchill as a thinker. His was thought for the sake of doing rather than thought for the sake of thinking, and wise leaders follow his example.

Fifth, Churchill was a lover. Few consider how essential love is to great leadership. Without love for causes and people, leadership grows unfocused and routine. But love infuses duty with energy, sets responsibilities in stark priority, and transforms labor into joyous sacrifice. Churchill understood this, and he allowed love to carry him to unusual levels of devotion and purpose. But his first loves were those nearest to him, and this is always the testing ground for love's genuineness. Once when Churchill was attending a formal banquet in London, some of the guests asked, "If you could not be who you are, who would you like to be?" Churchill thought for a moment. Surely he would say Napoleon, or his father, or even his ancestor, the first Duke of Marlborough. But at length Churchill responded: "If I could not be who I am," he said, taking his wife's hand, "I would most like to be Mrs. Churchill's second husband." Friends knew it was true, for Churchill was a romantic who loved with an irrational tenderness and loyalty. Without it—without a strength of love that moved him beyond himself—Churchill would never have been lifted beyond the self-centered and the common to genuine greatness.

Sixth, Churchill was a doer. A great deal that passes for leadership is actually carefully cultivated style. Style is its own reward, but true leaders have to be doers. Doers focus on results, outcome, and impact. Stylists focus on process, opinion, and image. Churchill was painfully aware of the problem of image over results in leadership, and in a speech to the St. George Society, he satirized what now routinely passes for political genius and effective leadership. His topic was how St. George might contend with his dragon in modern times. "St. George would be accompanied, not by a horse, but a delegation," Churchill wrote. "He would be armed not with a lance, but by a secretariat." St. George "would propose a conference with the dragon—a Round Table conference—no doubt that would be more convenient for the dragon's tail." "Then after making a trade agreement with the dragon, St. George would lend the dragon a lot of money." "The maiden's release would be referred to the League of Nations of Geneva and finally St. George would be photographed with the dragon." Churchill saw it clearly: doers get results while stylists expend their energies posturing. One is leadership; the other is entertainment.

Finally, Churchill was a giver. "We make a living by what we get," he once said, "but we make a life by what we give." Leaders must inherently be givers. They cannot afford to think first in terms of personal benefit since leadership for individual gain alone is not leadership, it is control. Somehow leaders have to believe, as Churchill did, that there are invisible laws that govern the universe and that those who give, position themselves to receive even more. Whether he called it sacrifice or duty or deserving victory, Churchill believed that the "mission of mankind" was for each generation to give so as to pass on more than it had received, to invest for another's return. As a historian, he also knew that a majority of the great leaders throughout history achieved their success only at the price of everything they had. Leadership, then, is about giving, and the mentality of the hireling and the profiteer has no place in the soul of leaders who strive to shape history as Churchill did. He made a life; others gathered their rewards, but gained only a living.

The chief lesson of Churchill's leadership is that greatness is a product of character, of matters like loyalty, sacrifice, endurance, and courage. Certainly Churchill accomplished many feats and the catalogue of his contributions to mankind may never be completed. But whether he was creating nations in the Middle East, anticipating the next threat to human freedom or writing histories to be read by a new generation, all his glory was but the by-product of exceptional character molded by a uniquely Christian understanding of the world.

It could be that when the final chapter of human history is written and Churchill is remembered from that distance, his greatest gift to succeeding generations may be found to have been this very issue of teaching men the price of greatness. There is some warrant for this expectation. More than a century and a half before Churchill was born, Blenheim Palace witnessed the performance of a special play in honor of the Duke of Marlborough. For the occasion, a local Bishop was asked to write a prologue in honor of the duke, who was to be in the audience for the much-anticipated event. The prologue amounted to a prophecy and almost three centuries later it is an astounding statement of the life of Churchill.

> *One shall arise who shall thy deed rehearse,*
> *Not in arched roofs, or in suspected verse;*
> *But in plain annals of each glorious year, With*
> *pomp of truth the story shall appear;*
> *Long after Blenheim's walls shall moulder'd lie,*
> *Or blown by winds, to distant countries fly,*
> *By him shall thy great actions all survive*
> *And by thy name shall his be taught to live.*[17]

Perhaps if men like Churchill are indeed remembered and heard in generations to come, it will mean nothing less than the inspiration to rise above the commonplace in the service of mankind. When this inspiration fills the hearts of leaders yet unborn and they seek to master the lessons of greatness, they will undoubtedly grow to revere the name and the life of Sir Winston Churchill.

Winston Churchill: The Lessons of Leadership

- Leadership is the power to shape the future.
- Bitterness erodes strong leadership: it anchors a leader to the past, distracting him from the promise of the future.
- Biology need not be destiny.
- A leader is often his own best teacher.
- Overwhelming moral and physical courage is at the foundation of all great leadership.
- Exceptional courage is born of a profound sense of destiny.
- To offer a people hope is to acquire a position of leadership in their lives.
- Religious faith elevates leaders by freeing them from the cult of the contemporary.
- The quality of a leader is often reflected in the quality of his marriage.
- Leadership is not a popularity contest; criticism is part of the job.
- Leaders are forged as much by time in the wilderness as by times of popularity.
- True leadership requires hard work–there is no substitute.
- The courage to look hard realities in the face is essential to effective leadership.
- A leader must see himself as the guardian of a heritage for future generations.
- A man cannot lead his generation if he cannot lead his children.
- Great leadership is held aloft by the winds of compassion.
- When a leader needs a break, a change is often as good as a rest.

- Men who believe in eternal life seldom fear death in this life.
- A sense of humor reflects a healthy grasp of the difference between what is and what ought to be.
- A leader will only command the level of loyalty he is willing to give to others.
- Great leaders apply the past to the present so as to shape the future.
- Words are the arsenal of leadership.
- Leaders can never afford to lose the beauty of life in the corrosive tedium of work.
- A firm grasp on eternal realities enables a leader to stand apart from his age and show it the way.
- The leader's task is to boldly confront the currents of change and harness its power for good.
- Great heights are only reached by overcoming great obstacles.

ENDNOTES

Prepages

1. All dates of published works in this chronology are from Frederick Woods' *Artillery of Words: The Writings of Sir Winston Churchill.*
2. All dates listed for the births of the Churchill children are from Mary Soames' *Clementine Churchill: The Biography of a Marriage.*

Section 1

1. *Churchill in Memoriam,* Staff of the New York Times (New York: Bantam Books, 1965), p. 78.
2. Marian Fowler, *Blenheim: Biography of a Palace* (London: Penguin Books, 1989), front cover.
3. Winston S. Churchill, *My Early Life* (New York: Charles Scribner's Sons, 1930), p. 4.
4. *Memoriam,* p. 83
5. William Manchester, *The Last Lion: Winston Spencer Churchill, Visions of Glory, 1874-1932* (Boston: Little, Brown and Company, 1983), p. 107.
6. Manchester, p. 107.
7. Ibid., p. 112.
8. *My Early Life,* p. 12.
9. Ibid., p. 12.
10. Ibid., p. 13.
11. Manchester, p. 127.
12. *My Early Life,* p. 13.
13. Ibid., p. 16.
14. Ibid.
15. Ibid., p. 17.
16. Ibid., p. 19.
17. Ibid., p. 60.
18. Manchester, p. 204.
19. *My Early Life,* p. 62.
20. Manchester, p. 215.
21. Ibid., p. 216.
22. *My Early Life,* pp. 83-84.
23. Ibid., p. 115.
24. *Memoriam,* p. 87.
25. *My Early Life,* pp. 225-226.
26. Ibid., p. 275.
27. Ibid., p. 280.
28. Ibid., p. 282.
29. Ibid., p. 283.
30. Ibid., p. 276.
31. John Pearson, *The Private Lives of Winston Churchill* (New York: Simon and Schuster, 1991), p. 105.
32. *Memoriam,* p. 93.
33. Manchester, p. 394.
34. Martin Gilbert, *Churchill: A Photographic Portrait* (New York: Wings Books, 1974), p. 117.
35. Martin Gilbert, *In Search of Churchill* (London: Harper Collins Publishers, 1994), p. 55.
36. Ibid., pp. 55-56.
37. Pearson, p. 151.
38. Ibid., p. 157.

39. Gilbert, p. 141.
40. *Memoriam*, p. 106.
41. Pearson, p. 224.
42. Piers Brendan, *Winston Churchill: A Biography* (New York: Harper & Row Publishers, 1984), p. 112.
43. Ibid., p. 126.
44. *Memoriam*, p. 115.
45. Ibid., p. 115.
46. Winston S. Churchill, *The Second World War: The Gathering Storm* (Boston: Houghton Mifflin Company, 1948), p. 665.
47. David Cannadine, ed., *Blood, Toil, Tears and Sweat: The Speeches of Winston Churchill* (Boston: Houghton Mifflin Company, 1989), p. 149.
48. Brendan, p. 153.
49. *Memoriam*, p. 39.
50. Winston Churchill, *Irrepressible Churchill, 1874-1965* (Cleveland: World Publishing Company, 1966), p. 252.
51. *Memoriam*, p. 120.
52. Ibid.
53. Ibid., p. 121.
54. Ibid., p. 122.
55. Ibid., p. 124.
56. Ibid., p. 128.
57. Brendan, p. 225.
58. Martin Gilbert, *Churchill: A Life* (New York: Henry Holt and Company, 1991), p. 959.

Section 2

1. William Manchester, *The Last Lion: Winston Spencer Churchill, Visions of Glory, 1874-1932* (New York: Little, Brown and Company, 1983), p. 188.
2. Randolph S. Churchill, *Winston S. Churchill: Youth, 1874-1900* (Boston: Houghton Mifflin Company, 1966), p. 43.
3. Martin Gilbert, *Churchill: A Life* (New York: Henry Holt and Company, 1991), p. 23.
4. Winston S. Churchill, *My Early Life: A Roving Commission* (New York: Charles Scribner's Sons, 1930), p. 46.
5. *My Early Life*, p. 46.
6. Ibid., p. 62.
7. Manchester, pp. 188-189.
8. Winston Churchill, *Irrepressible Churchill, 1874-1965* (Cleveland: World Publishing Company, 1966), p. 314.
9. *My Early Life*, p. 13.
10. Ibid., p. 12.
11. Ibid., p. 59.
12. Ibid., p. 111.
13. Randolph S. Churchill, p. 322.
14. Ibid.
15. Manchester, p. 242.
16. James C. Humes, *The Wit and Wisdom of Winston Churchill* (New York: Harper Collins Publishers, 1994), p. 23.
17. Winston S. Churchill, *Maxims and Reflections* (New York: Barnes and Noble Books, 1994), p. 33.
18. Manchester, p. 378.
19. Charles Eade, ed., *Churchill by His Contemporaries* (London: The Reprint Society, 1953), p. 168.
20. *Maxims and Reflections*, p. 175.
21. Manchester, p. 121.
22. Humes, p. 2.
23. Ibid., p. 47.
24. Ibid., p. 72.
25. Ibid., p. 2.
26. Ibid., p. 72.
27. *Irrepressible Churchill*, 109.
28. Winston S. Churchill, *Thoughts and Adventures* (New York: W. W. Norton & Company, 1990), p. 214.
29. Pearson, p. 133.
30. David Cannadine, ed., *Blood, Toil, Tears and Sweat: The Speeches of Winston Churchill* (Boston: Houghton Mifflin Company, 1989), p. 154.
31. Winston S. Churchill, *A History of the English Speaking Peoples: The New World* (New York: Dorset Press, 1956), p. 152.

32. Manchester, p. 430.
33. Pearson, p. 134.
34. Oskar Rabinowicz, *Winston Churchill on Jewish Problems* (Westport CT: Greenwood Press, 1974), p. 25.
35. Pearson, p. 284.
36. *My Early Life*, p. 28.
37. Pearson, p. 26.
38. Pearson, p. 156.
39. Pearson, p. 20.
40. Martin Gilbert, *Churchill: A Photographic Portrait* (New York: Wings Books, 1974), p. 18.
41. Winston S. Churchill, *Thoughts and Adventures*, (New York: W. W. Norton & Company, 1990), p. 7.
42. Humes, p. 187.
43. Pearson, p. 155.
44. Manchester, p. 25.
45. Pearson, p. 102.
46. Pearson, p. 418.
47. Winston S. Churchill, *The Second World War: The Gathering Storm* (Boston: Houghton Mifflin Company, 1948), p. 667.
48. Manchester, p. 401.
49. Pearson, p. 126.
50. Manchester, p. 400.
51. Ibid., p. 401.
52. *My Early Life*, p. 372.
53. Ibid., pp. 191-192.
54. *Churchill in Memoriam*, (New York: Bantam Books, 1965), p. 157.
55. Maxims and Reflections, p. 42.
56. Humes, p. 24.
57. Merle Miller, *Plain Speaking: An Oral Autobiography of Harry S. Truman* (New York: Berkley Publishing Corporation, 1973), pp. 26-27.
58. Humes, p. 24.
59. Ibid.
60. Report on the War, House of Commons, September 30, 1941.
61. *My Early Life*, p. 232.
62. Humes, p. 74.
63. *Irrepressible Churchill*, p. 100.
64. *My Early Life*, p. 67.
65. *Thoughts and Adventures*, p. 23.
66. Radio Broadcast to America on receiving the honorary Doctor of Laws degree from University of Rochester, New York, June 16, 1941.
67. *Memoriam*, p. 136.
68. Ibid., p. 120.
69. Humes, p. 31.
70. National Public Radio.
71. Humes, p. 36.
72. *My Early Life*, p. 5.
73. Manchester, p. 568.
74. Ibid.
75. Quoted in Martin Forbes, *History Lessons: The Importance of Cultural Memory* (New York: Palamir Publications, 1981), p. 61.
76. Winthrop Hudson, *Religion in America* (New York: Charles Scribner's Sons, 1973), p. 1.
77. *National Geographic*, August 1965, "Be Ye Men of Valour," p. 175.
78. *Maxims and Reflections*, p. 168.
79. *Memoriam*, p. 151.
80. Address at Harrow School, October 29, 1941.
81. Speech at the Lord Mayor's Day Luncheon, November 10, 1942.
82. Humes, p. 96.
83. Ibid., p. 23.
84. Ibid., p. 46.
85. Gilbert, *Churchill: A Photographic Portrait*, p. 199.
86. Ibid., p. 229.
87. Ibid., p. 234.
88. Winston S. Churchill, *Great Contemporaries* (New York: W. W. Norton and Company, 1990), p. 83.

89. Humes, p. 76.
90. Ibid., 50.
91. *Irrepressible Churchill,* p. 1.
92. Eade, p. 296.
93. Manchester, p. 34.
94. Ibid., p. 382.
95. *My Early Life,* p. 102.
96. Humes, p.163
97. Ibid., p. 308.
98. Pearson, p. 111.
99. Manchester, pp. 33-34.
100. Ibid., p. 384.
101. *Irrepressible Churchill,* p. 12.
102. Address at Harrow School, October 29, 1941.
103. Manchester, p. 184.
104. Ibid., p. 24.
105. Ibid., p. 23.
106. Ibid., pp. 758-759.
107. Brendan, p. 208.
108. *Thoughts and Adventures,* p. 10.
109. Humes, p. 20.
110. Gilbert, *Churchill: A Photographic Portrait,* p. 141.
111. *Maxims and Reflections,* p. 41.
112. *Irrepressible Churchill,* p. 121.
113. *My Early Life,* p. 93.
114. *Maxims and Reflections,* p. 35.
115. Ibid., p. 42.
116. *My Early Life,* p. 4.
117. Manchester, p. 786.
118. Ibid.
119. Humes, p. 19.
120. John Pearson, *The Private Lives of Winston Churchill* (New York: Simon and Schuster, 1991), p. 158.
121. Ibid., p. 353.
122. Ibid., p. 95.
123. Ibid., p. 84.
124. Ibid., p. 81.
125. Humes, p. 59.
126. Pearson, p. 128.
127. Manchester, p. 22.
128. Gilbert, *Churchill: A Photographic Portrait,* p. 35.
129. Humes, p. 88.
130. *My Early Life,* p. 73.
131. Ibid., p. 260.
132. Pearson, pp. 128-129.
133. Manchester, p. 22.
134. Humes, p. 7.
135. Pearson, p. 343.
136. Marian Fowler Blenheim: *Biography of a Palace* (London England, Penguin Books, 1989), p. 56
137. Robbin Fedden, *Churchill and Chartwell,* (Hampshire: The National Trust, 1990), p. 11.
138. Ibid.
139. Ibid., p. 12.
140. Ibid., p. 14.
141. Humes, p. 35.
142. Humes, p. 90.
143. Manchester, p. 36.
144. Ibid., p. 38.
145. Pearson, p. 388.
146. *My Early Life,* p. 127.
147. Manchester, p. 18.
148. Ibid., p. 36.
149. Ibid., p. 778.

150. Ibid., p. 24.
151. *Thoughts and Adventures*, p. 216.
152. Ibid.
153. Ibid., p. 217.
154. Ibid.
155. *Thoughts and Adventures*, p. 217.
156. Ibid., p. 220
157. Ibid.
158. *My Early Life*, p. 17.
159. Ibid., pp. 16-17.
160. Ibid., p. 17.
161. American Heritage, *"The Lion Caged,"* February-March, 1987, p. 84.
162. Manchester, p. 261.
163. Ibid., p. 30.
164. James C. Humes, *The Sir Winston Method* (New York: William Morrow and Company, Inc., 1991), p. 57.
165. Humes, p. 33.
166. Manchester, p. 31.
167. Pearson, p. 109.
168. Ibid.
169. Ibid.
170. Manchester, p. 32.
171. Ibid., p. 170.
172. *National Geographic*, p. 175.
173. *National Geographic*, p. 159.
174. Pearson, p. 379.
175. Ecclesiastes 5:19, KJV.
176. Randolph S. Churchill, p. 189.
177. Pearson, 138.
178. Pearson, p. 111.
179. Manchester, p. 376.
180. Gilbert, *Churchill: A Photographic Portrait*, p. 152.
181. Humes, p. 78.
182. Martin Gilbert, *In Search of Churchill* (Hammersmith: Harper Collins Publishers, 1994), p. 29.
183. *My Early Life*, p. 276.
184. Gilbert, *Winston Churchill: A Life*, p. 663.
185. Ibid., p. 599.
186. *Irrepressible Churchill*, p. 49.
187. Gilbert, *Winston Churchill: A Life*, p. 92.
188. *My Early Life*, p. 282.
189. Manchester, p. 173.
190. *Irrepressible Churchill*, p. 343.
191. Manchester, p. 176.
192. Mary Soames, *Clementine Churchill* (Boston: Houghton Mifflin Company, 1979), p. 395.
193. Ibid., p. 24.
194. *My Early Life*, p. 5.
195. Randolph S. Churchill, p. 207.
196. Manchester, p. 157.
197. Ibid, p. 231.
198. Ibid.
199. William Manchester, *The Last Lion: Winston Spencer Churchill, Alone, 1932-1940* (Boston: Little, Brown and Company, 1988), p. 233.
200. Humes, p. 56.
201. Pearson, p. 309.
202. Humes, p. 96.
203. *Blood, Toil, Tears and Sweat*, p. 177
204. *Maxims and Reflections*, p. 33.
205. Manchester, p. 11.
206. Ibid. p. 12.
207. Humes, p. 44.
208. Ibid., p. 12.
209. John Pollock, *Billy Graham* (Grand Rapids: Zondervan Publishers, 1966), p. 131.

210. *Thoughts and Adventures*, p. 209.
211. Randolph S. Churchill, *Winston S. Churchill: Young Statesman, 1901-1914* (Boston: Houghton Mifflin Company, 1967), p. 787.
212. *The Wit and Wisdom of Winston Chruchill*, p. 92
213. Humes, p. 40.
214. Ibid., p. 57.
215. Ibid., p. 55.
216. *Blood, Toil, Tears and Sweat*, p. 178
217. Speech to the Eighth Army at Tripoli [February 3, 1943].
218. Speech at the Lord Mayor's Day Luncheon, London [November 10, 1942].
219. *Blood, Toil, Tears and Sweat*, p. 177.
220. Ibid.
221. *Maxims and Reflections*, p. 104.
222. Humes, p. 44.
223. Ibid.
224. Humes, p. 40.
225. Humes, p. 24.
226. Ecclesiastes 7:2 (NIV).
227. Churchill, *My Early Life*, pp. 37-38.
228. Manchester, Vol. 1, p. 177
229. Humes, p. 25.
230. Gilbert, *Churchill: A Life*, p. 903.

Section 3

1. *Finest Hour*, Number 82, (1949), p. 5.
2. Richard Nixon, *Beyond Peace* (New York: Random House, 1994), p. 126.
3. Ibid, p., 16.
4. James Dale Davidson and Lord William Rees-Mogg, *The Great Reckoning* (New York: Simon and Schuster, 1993), p. 112.
5. Ibid., p. 109.
6. Bob Woodward, *Agenda: Inside the Clinton White House* (New York: Simon and Schuster, 1994), p. 190.
7. John Naisbitt, *Global Paradox* (New York: William Morrow and Company, Inc., 1994), p. 42.
8. Piers Brendan, *Winston Churchill: A Biography* (New York: Harper & Row, Publishers, 1984). p. 225.
9. John Pearson, *The Private Lives of Winston Churchill* (New York: Simon and Schuster, 1991).
10. CBS News Special Report, April 27, 1994 (Burrell's Information Services).
11. Oskar Rabinowicz, *Winston Churchill on Jewish Problems* (Westport: Greenwood Press, 1974), p. 25.
12. Winston S. Churchill, *Thoughts and Adventures* (New York: W. W. Norton & Company, 1990), p. 214.
13. Ibid., pp. 213-214.
14. Rabinowicz, p. 25.
15. Ibid., p. 21
16. Charles Eade, *Churchill by his Contemporaries* (London: The Reprint Society, 1953), pp. 326-327.
17. *Irrepressible Churchill*, p. 350.